KU-026-610

Supporting Schools

edited by
Colleen McLaughlin
and
Martyn Rouse
Cambridge Institute of Education

David Fulton Publishers
London

David Fulton Publishers Ltd
2 Barbon Close, London WClN 3JX

First published in Great Britain by
David Fulton Publishers 1991

Note: The right of contributors to be identified as the authors of their work has been asserted by them in accordance with the Copyright, Designs and Patents Act 1988.

Copyright © David Fulton Publishers Ltd

British Library Cataloguing in Publication Data

Supporting schools.
  I. McLaughlin, Colleen   II. Rouse, Martyn
  371

ISBN 1-85346-147-4

All rights reserved. No part of this publication may be reproduced, stored in a retrieval system or transmitted, in any form, or by any means, electronic, mechanical, photocopying, recording or otherwise, without the prior permission of the publishers.

Typeset by Chapterhouse, Formby L37 3PX
Printed in Great Britain by BPCC Wheaton Exeter.

Contents

Acknowledgements

Our thanks go to all the contributors to this book. Their work has been instrumental in the development of innovative practice in this field.

Thanks also go to past and present students on the Cambridge Institute of Education course 'Advice and Support'. Their active participation in, and contributions to, the debate have supported our development and thinking and have led in no small way to the birth of this book.

Contributors

Jan Campbell is an advisory teacher for personal and social education for Hertfordshire Country Council.

Susan Hart is a tutor at the Cambridge Institute of Education.

David Hopkins is tutor in curriculum studies at the Cambridge Institute of Education.

Colleen McLaughlin is a tutor in personal and social education at the Cambridge Institute of Education.

Jenny Reeves is adviser for special educational needs in the London Borough of Harrow.

Martyn Rouse is tutor in special educational needs at the Cambridge Institute of Education.

Ken Shooter was, at the time of writing, general inspector for design and technology for Cambridgeshire Country Council.

Mel West is a tutor at the Cambridge Institute of Education.

Preface

This book arose out of a Cambridge Institute of Education course entitled 'Advice and Support'. The course evolved as a result of requests from local education authorities, schools and teachers, for induction and training for the growing numbers of professionals whose new roles involved them in supporting school development. It also came about as a result of shifts in the educational, economic and political climate in which inspection, advisory and support services now find themselves operating. The professionals who work in these services are increasingly recognising that their future roles are uncertain. Indeed, current attempts to privatise the inspection of, as well as the support for, schools will involve a massive reappraisal of the nature, purpose and future of these services. This book attempts to bring together different strands of advice and support into one place so that lessons may be learned from existing good practice.

The book is intended for those professionals who are concerned with developing the educational experiences of all children through improving schools. This includes all those with advisory roles; inspectors, advisers, advisory teachers, educational psychologists, curriculum development officers and external consultants. In addition, there are an increasing number of teachers based in schools who are concerned with curriculum and staff development. Many of the lessons which have been learned about school improvement and the management of change are as relevant to insiders as they are to outsiders. It is not necessary to explain in detail at this stage the content of each chapter contained in this book. However, the main themes are:

- school development and the management of change;
- the nature of advisory and development work;
- the management of the role and evaluation of the work;
- the skills and processes involved;
- speculation about the future.

Any discussion about the future of this work is bound to be speculative. Changes in the educational, economic and political context have a profound impact upon expectations, structures, systems and roles. However, successful work in such a changing climate will depend upon our ability to preserve and develop aspects of positive practice which are currently in place. Much has been learned in the last decade or so about teacher development and school improvement. The book attempts to build upon this existing good practice in supporting schools.

Colleen McLaughlin
Martyn Rouse
Cambridge
October 1991

CHAPTER 1

School improvement and the problem of educational change

David Hopkins

In the course of my work I often talk with policy makers (by this I mean anyone who formulates and disseminates educational ideas, be they politicians, civil servants, LEA officers, heads, co-ordinators and so on) about the educational changes they wish to make. They often talk about these changes in the most concrete of terms, as if the change was an artefact we could see, touch and feel. In these conversations I am reminded of the story of the emperor's clothes. I often want to ask the 'policy makers' to let me see how their change works; to put the change artefact onto a trolley and wheel it into a school. When in my imagination they do this something very odd happens to the change, it begins to lose its shape and definition. By the time it approaches the classroom door the change has virtually disappeared, and when the trolley enters the classroom the change has vanished altogether. The reason being, of course, that at the classroom level educational changes are rarely tangible objects, they are more usually reflected in the different ways in which teachers and pupils work together.

Unfortunately this perspective is all too often lost on policy makers imbued with a more instrumental and concrete view of educational change. It is almost always the case that bureaucratic or 'top-down' change implicitly assumes that implementation is an event rather than a process: that it proceeds on 'auto pilot'. Centralised policy initiatives are rarely implementation friendly and their outcomes are consequently uneven.

The problem of change

This illustration raises for me one of the central problems of change: how do we translate policy into practice? Let me expand briefly on this point by looking at two related issues.

The first point is that in many change efforts the multi-dimensional character of implementation is often neglected. There are five commonly agreed components of implementation:

- organisation
- materials
- knowledge
- behaviour and role
- beliefs

The more these components are taken account of in a change of strategy the more likely it is that the innovation will succeed. Unfortunately this is rarely the case.

Secondly, the neglect of these components is related to a similar omission on the part of policy makers to consider the individuals' experience of change. School improvement is essentially a process whereby individuals alter their ways of thinking and doing. Fullan (1985) suggests that this implies that:

- change takes place over time
- change initially involves anxiety and uncertainty
- technical and psychological support are crucial
- the learning of new skills is incremental and developmental
- organisational conditions within and in relation to the school make it more or less likely that school improvement will occur
- successful change involves pressure and support

The neglect of attention on the part of policy makers to the components of implementation, and a lack of appreciation of the individual experience of innovation contribute to the central problem of change. Given this situation, which is becoming increasingly common in these days of centralised educational initiatives, what can those in and close to the school do to overcome the problem of change?

In this paper I suggest three broad strategies that advisory staff in LEAs, in particular, can use to facilitate the process of school improvement at the local level. These are:

- building an infrastructure for school improvement
- understanding the change process

- school development planning

Build an infrastructure for school improvement

Over the past five to ten years we have learned a great deal about the process of school improvement. School improvement was defined in the OECD sponsored International School Improvement Project (ISIP) as (Van Velzen in Hopkins 1987:1)

> a systematic, sustained effort aimed at change in learning conditions and other related internal conditions in one or more schools, with the ultimate aim of accomplishing educational goals more effectively.

The important emphasis is on the *process* as well as the *object* of change. This contrast was articulated notably by Seymour Sarason (1982) with his seminal *Culture of the School and the Problem of Change*. It is the quality of the school's internal processes, the way in which teachers teach, the structures and frameworks developed for curriculum and staff development, the spirit of collaboration and high expectations, in a word, the school's ethos that creates the conditions for student achievement. It is this that gives school improvement its distinctive character.

One of the major tasks of the school's support personnel is to help build an ethos that supports school improvement. This ethos was first described by Michael Rutter and his colleagues (1979) in their book *Fifteen Thousand Hours*. They attributed the significant differences in student outcomes achieved in broadly similar schools to the influence of the school's ethos. They wrote (Rutter et al 1979: 178):

> ... The differences between schools in outcome were systematically related to their characteristics as social institutions. Factors as varied as the degree of academic emphasis, teacher actions in lessons, the availability of incentives and rewards, good conditions for pupils, and the extent to which children were able to take responsibility were all significantly associated with outcome differences between schools. All of these factors were open to modification by the staff, rather than fixed by external constraints.

This line of research, into the characteristics of the effective school, has been extensively pursued in recent years (for a UK review see Reynolds 1985). Most of these studies have served to support the broad characterisation described by Rutter.

I would like to suggest that this 'ethos' is developed in part through the building of an infra-structure for change at and around the school level. What I mean by infrastructure are the strategies, frameworks and activities that schools and teachers use to support the change process. In Figure 1.1 I have identified some aspects of this infrastructure. The point is that it is the *integration* of these activities that is important, rather than the contribution of individual elements. In school improvement, as with many other things, the whole is greater than the sum of its individual parts.

The elements of the infrastructure provide a more concrete focus for the work of advisory and support staff. It is through the establishing of such structures and the ethos described by Rutter that it is sustained and generated. There are six components that contribute to this infrastructure: effective teaching, curriculum development, INSET, external support, teacher appraisal and school review and evaluation. Each of these activities requires a book for itself, so the following brief remarks serve merely to amplify the headings.

Although the term *effective teaching* is self explanatory, it is often the case that teaching strategies take second place to curriculum content. In a situation, however, where curricula are being increasingly imposed by central authorities, there is at least the opportunity for teachers to be more selective in the use of teaching strategies. It is now evident that the content of a lesson notwithstanding, the use of appropriate teaching strategies can dramatically increase student achievement (Joyce & Showers 1988). A major goal of school improvement is to develop teachers who are so professionally flexible that they can select, from a repertoire of models, the teaching approach most suited to a particular content area and their students' age and ability (Joyce & Weil 1986).

Despite the increasing centralisation of curriculum content, the task of *curriculum development* continues to present a major challenge. All too often curricular specifications appear in a form that teachers find difficult to use (Stenhouse 1975). Consequently, the responsibility for curriculum development is unwittingly devolved towards the school. Unfortunately, such specifications are often contradictory. The difficulties of relating academic content to whole curriculum issues, cross-curricular themes and skill based approaches are often unresolved by central authorities. Teachers rarely have the time to do such complex curriculum development. Advisers can play a central role in providing such support and by doing the analysis so necessary in making sense of recent curriculum advice.

The *inservice training of teachers* has for some time been recognised as a pre-condition for school improvement. Concerns over the 'match' between teachers' inservice needs and course provision has always

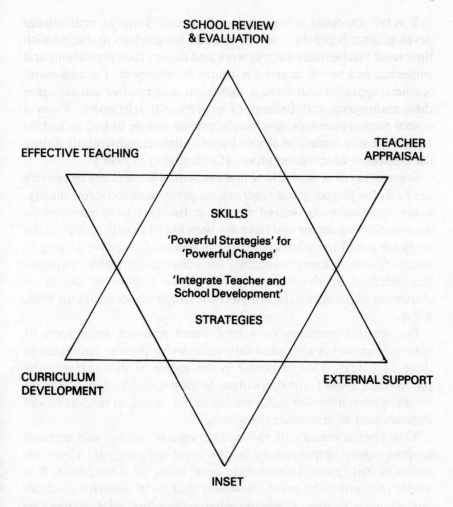

SCHOOL REVIEW
& EVALUATION

TEACHER
APPRAISAL

EFFECTIVE TEACHING

SKILLS

'Powerful Strategies' for
'Powerful Change'

'Integrate Teacher and
School Development'

STRATEGIES

CURRICULUM
DEVELOPMENT

EXTERNAL SUPPORT

INSET

Figure 1.1   Infrastructure for school improvement.

been problematic. The recent devolution in many countries of responsibility and funding for INSET to the school level has been an attempt to overcome this difficulty (Hopkins 1986). Such moves have, however, tended to result in short-term 'quick-fix' INSET with insufficient attention being given to embedding a system of professional development within the school's organisation. What is needed is timetabled INSET instead of supply cover, a commitment to peer-coaching on specific innovations rather than wide ranging one-shot workshops, and strategic ongoing support from advisers.

Teacher appraisal is regarded as a specific form of professional development. It provides an opportunity for teachers to discuss with their head teacher their current work and career, their aspirations and concerns, and to set targets for future development. For individual teachers appraisal can have a significant and positive impact upon their enthusiasm and feelings of professional self worth. From a school improvement perspective, appraisal can be linked to and be supportive of a variety of school based initiatives, particularly during the classroom observation phase. (Bollington *et al* 1990.)

Some form of *school review and evaluation* is necessary to provide the basis for planning and feedback on performance. Unfortunately, many approaches to school review in the past have assumed an accountability purpose and have not been linked closely enough to the everyday life of the school (Clift 1987). Although there are a range of school review strategies available, for school improvement purposes they need to be developmental, formative and linked closely to classroom practice and the everyday life of the school (Hopkins 1988, 1989).

Despite this emphasis on school based activities some form of *external support* is also necessary in order to provide assistance in these key areas. This of course is the theme of this chapter. The provision of INSET, the curriculum development function, and so on are all opportunities for those outside of the school, to support school improvement efforts inside the school.

This brief summary of the components of an infrastructure to support school improvement is of course not original. These are activities that 'good' schools have been doing for a long time. It is worth reiterating the point, however, that to be effective a school improvement strategy needs to combine the *object* of a change (the innovation) and a *process* whereby this innovation is to be implemented. If such an infrastructure is in place, then the process of implementation will be made all that much easier.

Understanding the change process

The infrastructure is about the pre-conditions at the school level for effective change and school improvement. This is different from the process involved in introducing innovation into the school. An understanding and monitoring of this process by advisers and support persons is a crucial aspect of their role as facilitators.

Once again, the last ten years have been a fruitful time for developing our knowledge about the change process. Amongst those who have contributed to this knowledge base are: Michael Fullan (1982, 1991); David Crandall and his colleagues (1983, 1986); and Michael Huberman and Matthew Miles (1984).

There is now a fair degree of consensus on the three major stages of the school improvement process: initiation, implementation and institutionalisation (see Figure 1.2).

Initiation	*Implementation*	*Institutionalisation*
Deciding to start	Carrying out action plans	Evaluating
Needs assessment	Developing commitment	Building in the process
	Time	

Figure 1.2   The school improvement process

Initiation is the phase of the innovation process where the decision is made to embark on a new programme or curriculum change. Although we may assume (with Fullan 1982:41) that 'specific educational changes are introduced because they are desirable according to specific educational values and meet a given need better than existing practices' this is not the way it always or even usually operates! Matthew Miles (1986) has recently made an analysis of the various stages of school improvement. Here is a summary of his list of factors that make for successful initiation:

- tie to a *local agenda* and high profile *local need*
- a clear, *well-structured approach to change*
- an active *advocate* or champion (LEA and/or school) who understands the innovation and supports it
- activate *initiation* to start the innovation (top down is OK under certain conditions *eg* with relatively small or specific changes)
- good *quality* innovation

Implementation is the phase of attempted use of an innovation. Implementation is a process, not an event; it involves people coming to terms and working with a new idea over a period of time.

As we have already seen, implementation is a complex process. This complexity is well illustrated in the factors affecting implementation, identified by Fullan (1981), given in Figure 1.3. Twelve factors are suggested as being critical to effective implementation; these factors tend to operate in a dynamic fashion, as a process over time, and form a system of variables which interact. If any one, two or three factors are working against implementation, the process will be less effective. Put more positively, the more factors supporting implementation, the more effective it will be. Space precludes a discussion of individual factors but their meaning and implication are reasonably self evident.

Factors affecting implementation

A   Characteristics of the innovation

    1   Need for the change
    2   Clarity and complexity of the change
    3   Quality and availability of materials

B   Characteristics at the school system level

    4   History of innovative attempts
    5   Expectations and training for head teachers
    6   Teacher input and professional development
    7   Governor and parental support
    8   Time line and monitoring
    9   Overload

C   Characteristics at the school level

    10   Head teachers' actions
    11   Teacher/teacher collaboration and actions

D   Factors external to the school system

    12   Role of DES, LEA and other educational agencies.

Figure 1.3   Factors affecting implementation

The key activities occurring during implementation are the carrying out of action plans, the developing and sustaining of commitment, the checking of progress and overcoming problems. The key factors making for success at this stage according to Miles (1986) are:

- clear responsibility for *coordination* (Head, Deputy, LEA officer, Coordinator)
- *shared control over implementation (top-down NOT OK)*; good cross-hierarchical work and relations; empowerment of both individuals and the school

- mix of *pressure*, insistence on *'doing it right'*, and *assistance*
- adequate and *sustained in-service support* both external and internal to the school
- *rewards for teachers* early in the process (empowerment, collegiality, meeting needs, classroom help, load reduction, supply cover, expenses, resources etc)

Institutionalisation: Until recently little attention had been paid to institutionalisation. It was assumed to happen automatically. Yet it was the case with many centralised initiatives that the innovations tended to fade away after the funding had ceased. In short, as Huberman and Crandall (quoted in Miles 1983:14) remark:

> In the chronicle of research on dissemination and use of educational practices, we first put our chips on adoption, then on implementation. It turns out that these investments are lost without deliberate attention to the institutional steps that lock an innovation into the local setting. New practices that get built in to the training, regulatory, staffing and budgetary cycle survive; others don't. Innovations are highly perishable goods. Taking institutionalisation for granted – assuming somewhat magically that it will happen by itself, or will necessarily result from a technically mastered, demonstrably effective project – is naive and usually self-defeating.

The move from implementation to institutionalisation often involves the transformation of a pilot project to a school wide initiative, often without the advantage of the previously available funding. It is change of a new order. Key activities at this stage involve an emphasis on 'embedding' which often implies changes in organisation, resourcing and the elimination of competing or contradictory practices. Miles' (1986) list of the factors making for success are:

- *organisational changes* supporting continuation 'embedding' the change.
- *tie-in to other change efforts, the curriculum and classroom instruction*
- *widespread use* in the school and LEA
- removal of *prior or competing practices*
- adequate bank of *local facilitators, advisory teachers* and skills

We have now looked at two broad approaches open to advisers in their work in supporting schools during the process of school improvement. The first was to help build the schools' infrastructure for change, and the second was to assist schools in becoming more expert at the process of change. This stands in contrast to much of the traditional work of advisers which has been content or subject based. These traditional strategies will not have had much of an impact unless they addressed the powerful organisational factors necessary for lasting school improvement. The focus of the advisers' work needs to be expanded and strengthened to incorporate fundamental and lasting organisational change. The two approaches just described are a start, but more specific strategies are needed which directly address the culture of the organisation. It is to a discussion of one of these powerful strategies that we turn in the following section.

School development planning

Current approaches to school development planning can in one sense be regarded as an extension of the more developmental school review activities of the early eighties. The GRIDS (Guidelines for the Review of Internal Development in Schools) project for example (McMahon *et al* 1984, Abbott *et al* 1988), outlined a practical developmental process based on an initial school review. We have recently found that GRIDS has been an effective strategy for a number of other initiatives, in particular teacher appraisal (Bollington and Hopkins 1989). Development planning, however, represents a more fundamental and comprehensive approach to school improvement that can incorporate both the process and object of change.

In their simplest form school development plans contain a set of curriculum and/or organisational targets with implementation plans and time-lines which reflects priorities set by the school on an annual basis within the context of local and national aims. The plans are usually based on a three year cycle with details for the first year and contingent aspirations for the subsequent two years. In many cases they also include details of performance indicators, staff development needs, organisational developments and resource implications.

In our booklet *Planning for School Development* (Hargreaves *et al* 1989: 4) we cite a number of advantages of development plans (DP). Among these are:

- a DP focuses attention on the aims of education, especially the learning and achievement, broadly defined, of all pupils
- a DP provides a comprehensive and co-ordinated approach to *all* aspects of planning
- a DP captures the long-term vision for the school within which manageable short-term goals are set
- a DP helps to relieve the stress on teachers caused by the pace of change
- the teacher's confidence rises
- the quality of staff development improves

The plan, of perhaps four to five pages, might include:

- the aims of the school
- the proposed priorities, the time-scale and who is involved
- the justification of the priorities in the context of the school
- the methods of reporting outcomes
- the broad financial implications of the plan

Once the plan is agreed, it needs to be turned into more detailed *action plans* with specific *targets* for the following year. These are the working documents for teachers.

It is easier to construct a development plan than to implement it. When the targets and success criteria are clear and specific, implementation and evaluation become easier. The targets and tasks establish what is to be done. The success criteria establish the basis for judging whether the targets have been met.

Many existing guidelines on school development planning describe implementation and evaluation as separate stages or phases. In some regards this is sensible: one cannot truly check on whether targets have been met until after implementation. The risk, however, is that schools may begin to ask themselves basic questions about evaluation late in their planning and so run into problems.

We therefore treat the processes of implementation and evaluation as interlaced, not as a period of implementation followed by 'big bang' evaluation at the end. If implementation and evaluation are linked, evaluation can help to shape and guide the action plan rather than being a *post mortem* upon it. Figure 1.4 provides an illustration of our integrated approach to implementation and evaluation.

Not all schools find development planning easy, and our more recent work on development planning (Hargreaves and Hopkins 1991) has attempted to explore this issue in more detail. In these cases we feel that more specific support from the advisory service may be needed.

In the current era of change schools now face a double problem. The first is that of development and change. Schools cannot remain as they are now if they are to implement recent reforms. For most schools this requires some adaptation. At the same time, schools also need to maintain some continuity with their present and previous practices. There is, therefore, for most schools, a tension between development (change) and maintenance (stability and continuity).

It is schools whose profile on the development-maintenance continuum tends towards the middle which will find it most easy to engage in development planning. Schools (or parts of schools) at the

12

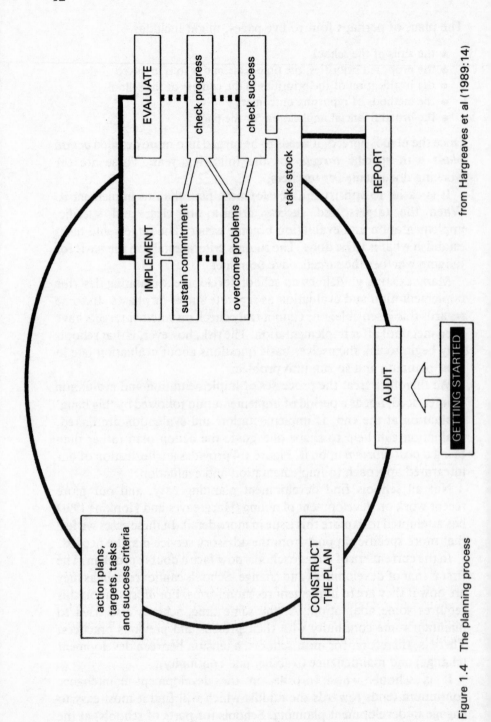

Figure 1.4 The planning process

from Hargreaves et al (1989:14)

development extreme may be so over confident in their innovative capacities that they take on too much too quickly. Schools at the maintenance extreme may either see little purpose in reform or have a poor record in managing innovation.

Despite this, schools have to innovate to generate the conditions to support other innovations. In terms of our metaphor of growth, the school with an extreme profile lacks roots (the preconditions) of sufficient strength to sustain the branches of innovation (eg the National Curriculum). Root innovations generate the base on which branch innovations can be sustained. Schools with a middle profile often tend to choose a blend of root and branch innovations. Schools at the extreme positions should be encouraged to do so.

So for example, at the construction phase, schools experiencing difficulties with development planning are most likely to lay foundations for future success when:

- the number of priorities chosen is very small
- there are both root and branch innovations
- branch innovations are restricted to those that cannot be postponed
- root innovations are selected to support the inescapable branch innovations

From the advisers' and support service point of view, development planning in these schools may require:

- as much protection as possible from pressure for innovation
- more support than other schools in the LEA

To be successful such support needs to be set within a mutually agreed strategy rather than consist of a series of individual tactics. A more strategic approach derives from a recognition that change is a relatively long-term process and that a carefully formulated step by step approach is to be preferred.

Particular attention should be given to the root innovations, since they are the foundation for the future branch innovations *and so make the school less dependent on LEA support in later years.*

This will require an alignment between the LEA's strategy for support and the school's slowly emerging strategy for its own development. Strategic alignment of this kind is likely to involve:

- *external pressure* without which the school may not move from its stable pattern of self-maintenance
- *external support* from the LEA in providing consultancy and protecting the school from too much pressure

- *internal pressure* the recognition by the governors, head and senior staff of the advantages of development to the school itself
- *internal support* the release of self-help and self-directing energy

When the focus in the initial stages is on root innovations, the school will be able to increase the number of branch innovations in later stages and thus increase its capacity to implement national and LEA policies successfully and to respond more effectively to unknown future demands for innovation and change.

Implications

In this chapter I have outlined what is for me the central problem of change – the lack of a perspective on the individual in the translation of policy into practice. In order for school improvement to occur as a result of centralised change we need to create conditions whereby individuals can interpret the meaning of an innovation to themselves in their own work situation.

This is particularly difficult to do at a time when so called 'top-down' approaches to change predominate. The contrast between 'top-down' and 'bottom-up' approaches, although superficially attractive, break down at the individual level. One person's 'bottom-up' approach may well appear to be 'top-down' to those who have to work with it. In one sense all change is externally initiated. Hence, the fundamental importance of the individual re-interpreting the innovation within the context of his or her educational world.

The task for the advisers is self evident, yet formidable. For it is they who have to assist in this process of re-interpretation. But, LEA support services are themselves in a period of change, as they clarify their own roles in the post-ERA period. So their task is doubly difficult. The trick seems to me to be able to develop a role that integrates the following two dimensions:

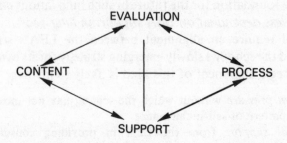

Figure 1.5   Dimensions of the advisory role

I realise that there are historical tensions in the conflation of these roles, yet unless this integration occurs the future of the support system, in its present form, may be short-lived.

It is for this reason that I have discussed in this paper some aspects of this new role. In particular: the creation of an infra-structure to support change at or near the school level; a more sophisticated appreciation of the change process; and the use of integrative and institution-focused strategies that directly address the culture of the school, such as school development plans. The challenge is as daunting as it is vital: for to paraphrase Michael Fullan (1988):

> Whatever the particulars, powerful strategies for powerful change are required, which restructure and integrate teacher and school development. It is no accident that long term school improvement strategies end up by integrating organisational research and curriculum issues. Without such integration the focus tends to be on the solutions themselves rather than the underlying problems.

Notes

1. This chapter is based on a paper given in Reggio Emilia, Italy in December 1989, at a conference sponsored by the Italian support agency for inservice teacher training (IRRSAE), Cassa Di Risparmio Di Reggio Emilia, and the OECD in Reggio Emilia, Italy in December 1989. The paper was subsequently published in Italian in the conference proceedings.
2. This section draws heavily on two of the publications from the DES funded *School Development Plans* project: *Planning for School Development* (Hargreaves et al 1989) and the *Management of Development Planning* (Hargreaves et al 1990).

References

Abbott, R. et al (1988) *GRIDS Handbook*, 2nd edn (Primary and Secondary School versions) York: Longman for the SCDC.

Bollington, R. and Hopkins, D. (1989) School Based Review as a Strategy for Implementation. *Educational Change and Development*, Vol 10, No 1, pp 8–17.

Bollington, R. et al (1990) *An Introduction to Teacher Appraisal*. London: Cassell.

Clift, P. et al (1987) *Studies in School Self Evaluation*. Lewes: Falmer Press.

Crandall, D. and Loucks, S. (1983) *A Roadmap for School Improvement*. Andover, MA: The Network Inc.

Crandall, D. et al (1986) Strategic Planning Issues That Bear on the Success of School Improvement Efforts. *Educational Administration Quarterly*, Vol 22, No 3, Summer, pp 21–53.

Fullan, M. (1982) *The Meaning of Educational Change*. Toronto: OISE Press.

Fullan, M. (1985) Change processes and strategies at the local level. *Elementary School Journal,* **85**, 3, pp 391–421.

Fullan, M. (1988) Change processes in secondary schools: Towards a more fundamental agenda. Toronto, University of Toronto, Faculty of Education (mimeo).

Fullan, M. (1991) *The New Meaning of Educational Change*. London: Cassell.

Fullan, M. and Park, P. (1981) *Curriculum Implementation*. Toronto, Ontario: Ministry of Education.

Hargreaves, D. H. et al (1989) *Planning For School Development*. London: DES.

Hargreaves, D. H. et al (1990) *The Management of Development Planning*. London: DES.

Hargreaves, D. H. and Hopkins, D. (1991) *The Empowered School*. London: Cassell.

Hopkins, D. (ed) (1986) *Inservice Training and Educational Development*. London: Croom Helm.

Hopkins, D. (ed) (1987) *Improving the Quality of Schooling*. Lewes: Falmer Press.

Hopkins, D. (1988) *Doing School Based Review*. Leuven. Belgium: ACCO.

Hopkins, D. (1989) *Evaluation for School Development*. Milton Keynes: Open University Press.

Huberman, M. and Miles, M. (1984) *Innovation Up Close*. New York: Plenum Press.

Joyce, B. and Weil, M. (1986) *Models of Teaching* (3rd edition). Englewood Cliffs: Prentice Hall.

Joyce, B. and Showers, B. (1988) *Student Achievement Through Staff Development*. New York: Longman.

McMahon, A. et al (1984) *The GRIDS Handbook* (primary and secondary school versions). York: Longman for the Schools Council.

Miles, M. (1983) Unravelling the Mysteries of Institutionalization. *Educational Leadership*. Vol 41, No 3, November, pp 14–19.

Miles, M. (1986) Research Findings on the Stages of School Improvement. Centre for Policy Research. New York (mimeo).

Reynolds, D. (1985) *Studying School Effectiveness*. Lewes: Falmer Press.

Rutter, M. et al (1979) *Fifteen Thousand Hours*. London: Open Books.

Sarason, S. (1982) *The Culture of the School and the Problem of Change*. 2nd edn., Boston, MA: Allyn and Bacon.

Stenhouse, L. (1975) *An Introduction to Curriculum Research and Development*. London: Heinemann Educational.

CHAPTER 2

Supporting change within schools: the development of advisory services

Jenny Reeves

In this chapter I want to look first at some of the major issues that arose for participants involved in a change process within the secondary school phase, then to discuss some means for tackling these and, finally, to look at the implications this has for the work of advisory and support services.

Introduction

A year ago I completed a study of my own work with five secondary schools over a three year period (1985–1988) whilst I was an advisory teacher for special educational needs (Reeves 1990). The study looked at my interactions with the schools from two viewpoints: my own perceptions and those of the special needs co-ordinators (SNCs), who were the people that I worked principally with. I also interviewed other advisory teachers about their perceptions of the role to see whether there were elements of commonality in the functions we undertook.

Although it may seem that the insights gained from exploring such an area are limited when it comes to the topic of supporting schools, there are certain features of working in the field of special needs in the late eighties which have a universal applicability.

Following the Warnock Report, there was a general drive to initiate whole school approaches to special needs in ordinary schools. In essence, this was about a transfer of responsibility for pupils with learning difficulties to mainstream staff (as opposed to special education staff) and the widening of each school's ability to make appropriate provision for students with special educational needs. This was to be achieved through the development of ordinary curricular provision to enable such students to have appropriate learning experiences so that they could participate in and benefit from the whole curriculum. Special education staff were to take the lead in promoting the innovation through working collaboratively with their colleagues in the classroom rather than withdrawing students for remedial work.

This gave special needs staff both outside and within schools a specific responsibility to bring about change. It is in focusing on the relationship between internal and external change agents that the results of the study have a wider applicability to the work of those engaged in supporting schools.

Making sense of the change

What emerged very clearly from the study was that both my school-based colleagues and I had a great deal in common when it came to the issues that confronted us as professionals and that this had more to do with sharing the change agency role than having the same 'subject' label.

The major problem that we experienced did not lie in knowing what we wanted to achieve in the long term – the 'should' of the innovation – but how to achieve it. This was underlined by the close match found in the study between the process functions of advisory teachers (e.g. personal support and backing, clarifying ideas, problem-solving) and those functions which school-based colleagues particularly valued.

The 'how' problem is one of answering such questions as: What would implementing the 'should' be? What would it look like? It is a problem of meaning and of translation into practicality (Fullan 1982). It was compounded considerably by the complexity of the number of subsystems that needed to be influenced in promoting 'whole-school' innovations: subject departments, senior management, pastoral structure, pupils, parents and governors.

This complexity means that the timescale for ensuring real entitlement to the whole curriculum for children with learning difficulties is certain, at best, to be lengthy. Many attitudes and practices need to be changed within the teaching profession as a whole and in society generally. Many people have to be mobilised and their energy and commitment in promoting the innovation has to be sustained. For each of these groups, and the individuals within them, the issue of meaningfulness arises and the change agents will have to work with them to find a basis which makes sense to both sides before and whilst they engage in the process of change.

The pain of change

Another key issue was that of discomfort and stress. The evidence indicated a high level of resistance to the changes and not all of it from expected sources. There was not simply the overt resistance from some colleagues which the SNCs gave witness to but also the resistance of incomprehension within the change agents themselves and therefore, between themselves and others, even when those others were committed to the innovation.

There is a personal struggle for those involved in the change process in continually having to confront their own ideas and actions and deal with the self-doubt to which this gives rise. Moving to the new often necessitates a breaking up of past beliefs and values (Perls et al 1951) and this process is seldom painless. Many of the staff concerned, including myself, came from a background of remedial work and we had developed our expertise in working with small groups of pupils outside the mainstream classroom. The innovation required a major change of attitude on our part and some 'negative' reappraisal of our past practices and experience.

The new school co-ordinator role demanded a set of skills, in terms of interacting and co-operating with other staff, for which SNCs, and advisory teachers coming from the same culture, were often ill-prepared. The fact that this is general in teaching which is marked by professional isolation (Mulford 1982, Hargreaves 1982) only served to exacerbate the problem.

Furthermore, the new role ran counter to the norms of the majority of secondary schools. There are few role precedents for working in class with other teachers. Discussing at a professional level the practice of teaching with colleagues has been largely 'taboo' (Hargreaves 1982). Traditionally, there is no legitimate basis for colleagues to be involved in or comment upon the work of any department other than their own. Evidence from both the advisory teachers and the SNCs showed that there was a great concern with issues of credibility in terms of influencing and working with colleagues from a variety of subject backgrounds.

The staff, who were required to operate as change agents and consultants, had the added difficulty of working in the interests of a student group whose very existence is often seen as an impediment to the efficient working of the school. Most of those who were being required to influence the whole system, therefore, had the added handicap of starting from a marginalised position within it.

Thus, the whole concept of the wider role envisaged for special needs staff was a major structural and psychological innovation and created a great deal of role conflict and ambiguity for postholders (Kahn et al in ed. Biddle & Thomas 1966). These problems are shared to a greater or lesser extent by anyone working as a change agent within an institution as well as by those trying to promote change from the outside.

All these factors gave rise to considerable stress which is not generally validated in the literature nor, in my experience, is it clearly articulated in the discussions of advisory and support staff. As we move people into accepting new roles and practices, we should be clearly aware of the tensions and anxieties that arise for them as a result.

Complexity and longevity

When an innovation is complex and long-term an obvious corollary is that it requires a great deal of energy and work on the part of the change agents and this can become overwhelming. There can often be a sense of getting nowhere when current practice falls far short of the ideal and where the conceptualisation of the change process is simplistic, a trap that all of those involved in the study fell into, including myself.

A complex innovation has a need to change the structures through which it is promoted. This presents a very real problem in that, if it is not understood, stagnation is very likely to occur, a natural outcome given the amount of energy needed by participants in order to achieve the changes required. Complexity and longevity raise the issue of redundancy which needs to be addressed continually if the process of implementation is not to be halted. A structure, approach or strategy which may have been appropriate at one stage of the process may actually be an impediment to a later stage of implementation. Unfortunately, in developing such a transitional arrangement, those involved have made a commitment and investment in the particular conceptualisation of the innovation that this represents. To move to the next phase they must now unpick this point of view, see their present practice in a critical light and be prepared either to modify or abandon all or part of it.

This was true of support teaching in the particular case study in which I was involved. Originally, we assumed that by simply moving special needs staff into ordinary classrooms curriculum development would follow. It did not and we had to rethink our approach.

Having looked at some of the issues involved in promoting complex whole school changes, I want to examine some of the ways in which these can be addressed.

Taking a broad view

There is a need to see an innovation and its implications in a holistic sense. In many ways current thinking does not encompass what the words 'whole school' really mean. To view whole-school initiatives as a matter of implementing a few structural changes is far too simplistic.

As change agents we need to take into account the totality of the field if we are to have an influence upon it. Too specialist and narrow a focus will not gain credibility with other staff, we have to learn to take account of their realities and their perceptions and be prepared to learn, modify and change our strategies in the light of this without ever losing sight of the ultimate aims of the innovation.

The outcomes of this process can be seen in the general changes in content as the innovation proceeds, which are linked to changes in the type of personnel involved and are a result of the trading off process and the need to widen the conceptual framework. In the case of the study, the first stage was very much about the broad content of the innovation, the aims and rationale; the second about changing structures (the settings and systems in which special needs staff worked); the third about managing working with others and curriculum generally; the fourth increasingly about learning and teaching styles and the process of change.

Similar changes can also be seen if one tracks the literature on special needs, where there is an increasing identification of effective provision for pupils with learning difficulties with the adoption of good educational practice.

There is a need to be opportunistic and flexible and to use any openings which the environment presents in order to further development. Current developments such as Technical and Vocational Education Initiative (TVEI) and the National Curriculum can have a strong influence on the general direction that the innovation takes and what are identified as content components. There is a constant need to 'colonise' other innovations and to use them to further long term aims. In adopting an eclectic framework participants will be open to seizing upon beneficial opportunities offered by the environment, thus maximising their effectiveness.

A further element in viewing an innovation holistically concerns the complexity of subsystems both within schools and the LEA. Looking at this in terms of involvement, the succession of staff in the study at school level could be represented very simplistically as:

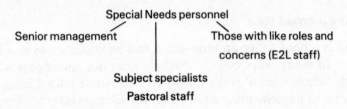

Figure 2.1   Levels of involvement

Within those categories some commonality of interests has to be found before the groups/individuals will be prepared to become involved and engage in promoting the innovation. Nor does this list represent a straightforward progression. Development has to proceed up and down the list. Structurally there seem to be a set of oscillations between the levels within the organisation at which changes take place. One can see that initially collaborative work can occur at a fairly low level in the hierarchy but that it will probably throw up issues which have implications for timetabling, resourcing and other institutional structures if the outcomes are to be put into practice on a wider scale. Equally, if new institutional structures are adopted, they will influence those staff lower down the hierarchy and have implications for the practice.

A similar set of oscillations between external and internal developments can also be seen e.g. in the influence of the TVEI group on individual members and hence on their institutions and contrariwise the influence on the work of the group of individual members. What this implies is that we should view educational change in a much more eclectic and systemic fashion rather than drawing false dichotomies between top-down, bottom-up, school-based and external INSET or being hidebound by a simple view of the operation of intra- and inter-institutional boundaries.

The action research cycle

One way in which the development of conceptualisation, knowledge and skills on the part of the change agents can be achieved is through doing, through taking action. In fact theoreticians would argue that this is the only way to achieve an understanding of complex change because none of the participants can know how implementation will proceed in detail from the beginning nor could such knowledge be derived *a priori* as there are too many variables to account for (Beckhard & Harris 1987).

This requires that participants gain a sense of achievement and progress as well as being given space to understand and make the changes meaningful and workable for themselves.

Thus, the innovation needs to be reduced to manageable proportions, to a series of stages where structures are formed which have potential for development and participants are enabled to become proactive and to experience success. If this is not done participants may well lose heart or feel overwhelmed from the outset.

A useful mechanism for doing this is the action research cycle which provides a basic process to follow (Lewin 1948). As change is necessarily about learning and the cycle of review, planning, action and evaluation is a good learning model, it gives change agents a powerful tool for facilitating development (Argyris & Schon in ed. Lockett & Spear 1980).

In part this element, of command over process, is being undertaken through Local Management of Schools with the promotion of the idea that schools should engage actively in forward planning and be looking to an action research cycle as a vehicle for developing school effectiveness (DES 1989). However, this still leaves the problem of actually implementing the planning cycle, which in many instances may require the assistance of outside agencies, until schools are more confident and versed in the process themselves.

In itself, guidance through a successful process of change by advisory and support staff is not sufficient. School-based participants need to attain command over the process for themselves so that they can function independently within their own institutions. There is some evidence from the study that where groups or individuals do acquire greater command over the process of change then development proceeds at a greater pace and they become less dependent upon support from outsiders.

I think it is useful to insert another phase in the action-research cycle vis a digestion/gestation period to allow for consolidation and recovery. This also avoids the trap of evaulating the effect of a course of action too simplistically. It may take a while before the full implications of a particular change can be fully understood.

It is also the case that because change requires a great deal of energy and effort there is a danger of overloading participants if the pace is too swift. Small achievable steps seem to provide the greatest success and encouragement although outsiders probably have a role in applying a further 'booting' pressure to move the innovation forward again after each cycle has been accomplished.

At this point there is a need to develop feedback and renewal mechanisms that will ensure that review and reflection take place. This is a key activity in the implementation process and one which it is easy either to ignore or to treat superficially. Because the path of implementation is impossible to specify precisely from the outset good feedback is absolutely vital if the process is to be managed effectively and blocks are to be confronted and overcome as and when they arise.

The ethos for change

One of the keys to effectively promoting renewal and continued implementation seems to be establishing a non-judgemental ethos where there is an acceptance of 'error' and 'failure'. What seems to be effective is adopting an experimental frame of mind where outcomes are viewed as neutral 'results' and hence, all are acceptable in hypothesis forming about what the next course of action should be. Such an ethos encourages the good feedback which is so essential to managing the change process by ensuring 'you get the news you don't want to hear' rather than going up a blind alley because no-one is prepared to provide information which appears to be negative.

Where participation is required and the innovation needs to be implemented in a variety of contexts it seems particularly important to adopt an acceptant approach. It is often tempting to rule out certain people/schools as a waste of time but the cost may well be a consequent lowering of morale and increase of resistance in the form of compliance and/or withdrawal (Smith 1980). In any case, winning over those who are initially opposed to the innovation is both politically expedient and trials the work of the innovators in that this must be a central task in order to ensure progress.

This raises the nature of the relationship between external and internal change agents. It seems essential that advisory staff recognise that their relationship with colleagues in school is one of mutuality and partnership. It is the teachers in school who carry out the bulk of the work in promoting an innovation and it is they alone who have essential information about the nuts and bolts of implementation. The role of advisory staff needs to be set clearly in that context rather than being seen as that of sole, or even prime, movers in relation to change.

Groups, teams and collegiality

One source of providing supportive and effective contexts for change which has often been underused by both internal and external change agents is that deriving from the information of groups and teams. There is still a strong tendency in educational change for people to function as lone 'hero innovators' which considerably reduces their effectiveness.

Interestingly, when I examined the evidence from the advisory teachers on the functions and activities they were involved in there was a high degree of matching with the taxonomies derived from looking at the work of other change agents (Miles, Saxl & Lieberman 1988, Mulford in ed. Gray 1988). However, one element was largely missing which was that of seeing themselves as working with groups and teams.

The study, as well as the literature on change, suggests that the formation of groups and teams can be a powerful factor in speeding up the implementation process. Groups, whether internal or external, can take over consultancy functions, just as the TVEI group in the study demonstrated by providing its members with elements of acceptant, catalytic and confrontational consultancy. This relates back to the theme of the pain of change and the need for support and validation. It may be that it is in providing psychological support, as much as the pooling and sharing of ideas and 'ownership', which makes a collaborative/collegial approach to complex change productive.

Applying pressure

Most human institutions have an in-built resistance to change and thus all change requires the application of pressure, either by internal or external forces (Handy 1985).

The corollary to the strength of the resistance encountered by the SNCs in the study was the high value that they placed on backing and support. This is particularly necessary where the changes which are being promoted do not simply affect a group who have a clear reason for identifying with the innovation. The requirement to implement whole school approaches adds to the resistance that is encountered, since it necessarily means that the innovators must proselitise and mobilise those who, initially, may see no reason to support the changes.

In addition to the pressure which groups and individuals can exert, is that which is applied through policies. The SNCs found the fact that the Local Education Authority (LEA) had adopted a policy on special educational needs and that the TVEI policy stressed the need of access for all pupils extremely useful to them. It legitimised their activities, provided a basis for questioning present practices with colleagues and validated changes in the way in which they were beginning to operate. Interestingly, it also gave them a basis for discounting total responsibility for innovations within their own settings (advisory and support staff can be used in the same way).

The application of pressure clearly does raise ethical problems and this is perhaps why terms such as 'needs identification', 'ownership' and 'support' are so popular in some quarters, because they disguise some of the issues that the use of pressure gives rise to.

To sum up all these elements: adopting a holistic framework, using action research, establishing an experimental/open ethos, working in groups and teams have implications for the external change agency. Advisory teams will need to plan, organise and control developments in relation to external support and do this in such a way that it allows for the empowerment of internal change agents so that they can bring about development in their own institutions.

Consultancy models

Looking at the evidence from the case study, there seems to be an overwhelming emphasis upon the need for expertise in relation to managing the process of change on the part of both the SNCs and the advisory teacher.

The closest analogue to these functions are those which are listed in works on consultancy (Argyris 1970). Looking at Schein's (1969) outline for the progress of process consultancy interventions, there are clearly parallels:

(1) Initial contact with the client organisation
(2) Defining the relationship, formal contact, and psychological contract
(3) Selecting a setting and a method of work
(4) Data gathering and diagnosis

(5) Interventions
(6) Reducing involvement
(7) Termination.

However, there are basic differences in the relationship of LEA advisory staff to schools and that of consultants employed directly by schools in that the former have a brief which extends beyond simply meeting the client's needs. Advisory staff have a responsibility to implement LEA policies and, therefore, cannot be viewed as neutral outsiders (Bolam et al 1978, Winkley 1986).

I also suspect that Schein's model presents an over-simplification of the realities of assisting to bring about complex change, although as a basic framework it has a great deal to recommend it. For instance, if each burst of activity with a particular school is considered as a single episode the model would broadly apply. However, this would miss out the on-going contacts between periods of intensive interaction and bias the picture towards seeing school-based intervention as something separate and distinct from other activities going on within the LEA, a viewpoint which I would argue that the evidence of the study calls into question.

Nevertheless, Schein's model can serve as a basis for making more explicit the reasons for any given intensive interaction with a particular school. Such periods could be better delineated in terms of the aims and objectives of the intervention so as to generate more explicit pre-planning. The notion of termination (step 7 above) is also extremely important. Seeing an end to a particular phase would assist in judging the effectiveness of interventions and provide a basis for collecting feedback so that participants can judge what has been achieved and how their work could be improved. It might, thus, begin to overcome the problem that many advisory staff experience, of not having criteria for judging success as well as providing a good basis for 'on-the-job' training.

A useful way of beginning to view the role over time is to mesh together the stages during the implementation of a change, the modes of consultancy identified by Blake & Mouton (in Bennis et al 1979) and the model of the nature of consultation developed by Schmuck (Murgatroyd and Reynolds 1984). Applying this to the evidence from the case study, the stages could be typified by those in Figure 2.2 below.

This tracks the original prime demand on the client/consultant relationship as being one of personal support and validation, moving to a stage where the paramount need is for developing ways and means of setting about taking action, followed by a next phase where there is

28

a need to reflect critically upon what is happening/has happened and to confront blocks.

CLIENT	MODE	NATURE
Stage 1 Establishing a Dialogue		
Individual	Acceptant	Consultative Assistance
Stage 2 Preparing for & Implementation Phase I		
Individual/group (external)	Acceptant	Content Consultation
	Catalytic	
Stage 3 Review and Implementation Phase 2		
Groups (internal & external)	Catalytic	Process Consultation
	Confrontational	
(Acceptant & catalytic functions increasingly taken over by groups.)		

Figure 2.2   Conceptual framework for supporting implementation

The outline in Figure 2.2 could begin to give us a possible conceptual framework for supporting implementation. However, for the reasons given above (p. 27), the task of empowering school-based personnel as change agents in their own right must be central.

What this implies is that those acting as external change agents need to have at their command a variety of consultancy styles, to recognise when and where their use is appropriate, and in addition to have a good understanding of the change cycle and how to implement it.

Knowledge linkage and problem-solving

Another important function of advisory and support staff is serving as a collecting point for information. Looking at my own contribution to the case study, there is evidence of the importance of having good information as a basis for problem-solving both in relation to the individual institution and in bringing to bear information from a variety of other sources.

In some senses this is less obvious to the staff in schools. However, looking at the evidence from the SNCs they do value having access to a range of possible strategies and the clarifying function which outsiders can perform through listening and helping them to sort out their ideas. The outsider status is important in that it provides a different point of perception, a distance from the day to day working of the school which can help staff to reframe issues and problems.

Again it is difficult to draw clear boundaries around this function because it overlaps with the next, which is networking. Here the advisory services can facilitate the formation of groups drawing membership from a number of institutions. This too can break down the parochialism of too school-based an approach by allowing for the exchange of information and strategies.

In addition, successful groups can serve as a source of pressure to keep the innovation going by encouraging members to try new approaches in their own institutions through knowing that their peers have used them. Network members can provide reassurance and detailed information on implementation which helps others to move forward and to avoid pitfalls. This also helps to move the innovation forward as the credibility of fellow practitioners, drawing on current experience, is higher than that of advisory and support staff using secondhand accounts.

What emerged from the study is that there is a danger of breakdown in the knowledge linkage role at the point of influencing other subject departments. The implications here are that other mechanisms may be needed to bridge the entry gap which both internal and external change agents experience. One problem of LEA advisory services is that they are to organise them purely upon subject lines, hard to avoid given the subject-based approach embodied in the National Curriculum. If advisory teachers for special needs worked collaboratively with their counterparts in other subject areas this would provide, both logically and practically, a better basis for penetration than working in isolation. The previous discussion on process issues would give a good basis for joint working as both this study and the literature would suggest that there is a great deal of commonality in the change agency role whatever the content of the innovation being promulgated by the innovators.

Again, by mounting in-service training which puts subject specialist and special needs staff together, the LEA could assist staff to develop professional relationships which would further the work in this area rather than targeting each group of staff separately.

Advocacy and leadership

Continuing with the theme of pressure, SNCs seemed to value particularly those occasions where the advisory teacher acted as an advocate and a defender for the internal change agent/s and her/their cause. I suspect that hidden within this is direct subject knowledge in the sense of knowing the ins and outs for arguing the case and being able to do so from the stance of an expert in the field. What the SNCs may be appreciating is the ability to demonstrate expertise to others as a form of persuasion/pressure even though they may not feel they need to call upon such expertise directly for themselves.

Another highly appreciated function is the ability of the external change agent to mobilise resources. This is linked to the defender role where the backing of the advisory teacher impinged upon senior management within the school to secure for example changes in time-tabling, staffing, opportunities for providing INSET, forming planning groups. Equally, this applied to securing resources from outside the school for curriculum development projects for example.

This last is particularly important. Targeting resources to allow individuals to work together on a task that has immediate practical outcomes and allows teachers actually to change their practice is essential. What emerged from the study was that linking resources to action in schools was very beneficial to ensuring progress. This is not an exclusive requirement, the study would indicate that there is a role for traditional INSET, but that learning by doing and reflecting upon action performs a vital part in the process of change and probably cannot be skimped (Joyce & Showers 1988, Fullan 1986).

This requires the exercise of a leadership function somewhere in the process (Bass 1980). There is a need to mobilise groups and individuals to achieve change. There is a need to define short term goals and ensure their achievement, to prioritise such goals and to target resources. There is a need to sustain motivation and involvement. Beyond these functions within the group of innovators there is also a need for skilful politicking, the changes that are required inevitably raise issues of status, power and control within schools and the LEA organisation. At this strategic level there will be a continuing need for the involvement of LEA personnel (Bolam 1984).

Implications for the advisory services

The case does suggest that a change agency view of the role should be taken by LEAs. I do not think that my own inclination to conceive the role in this way wholly influenced the SNCs to express such a clear need for assistance in coping with the change process. Clearly, this has implications for the kind of training and support that advisory teachers need to carry out their work effectively.

The other implication is that in order to promote whole school approaches the LEA needs to have a whole advisory approach towards implementing the changes in schools as it is neither logical nor feasible for advisory staff with a special needs brief to work on their own. Just as SNCs in school cannot promote real curriculum change by working in isolation so, for advisory staff, the strategy must be collaborative. Traditional boundaries based upon a subject-specific viewpoint have to be breached and this will be better done by an advisory service which has itself had experience of collaborative work than by one which mirrors the subject divisions (Kloska in ed. Ramasut 1989).

As to the precise functions of the advisory teacher, I find this more difficult to delineate. What I think emerges from the study is some clarification of the kind of functions that need to be performed by advisory and support services but, since the study did not compare and contrast the work of other external staff working with schools, it is not possible to throw a great deal of light upon who should do what.

What it may point to is that different functions need to be performed at different stages in development. For example, at the point of developing curriculum, a collaborative approach within the advisory service may well be more effective than one which leaves each specialist 'going it alone' although the latter, targeting specific staff, may be effective during early stages of development. I think though that I would still argue that working together with other advisory staff in specifically developing the change agency role would have helped me considerably in carrying out my work.

Because of the high level of resistance I believe that the training of change agents, both external and internal, needs to be thorough and to continue as they engage in the work. The training programme should focus on developing an understanding of the change process and the skills required to bring about change as well as knowledge about the nature of the innovation. External change agents need to be aware of the stress their colleagues face in schools and to use supportive methods and structures which ease negative effects.

There are also the changes which may be required on the part of external staff as school-based colleagues develop greater independence. Providing close-coupled personal support may well become less salient if internal staff become more self-confident and part of effective teams and networks.

The evidence from the study also implies that less emphasis needs to be placed upon traditional INSET which centres round ideas and attitudes and a much greater emphasis centred on INSET which is action orientated. As part of this change of strategy more backing needs to be provided for work in schools *as it takes place* and for those working as outsiders to use the feedback from such initiatives in net-working between staff from different schools.

Fulfilling this role will require that advisory and support staff are fairly close-linked to their school-based colleagues in order to be responsive to the needs that arise during implementation phases. Despite this close linkage, they will need to retain their outsider view-point. It can happen that advisory staff simply accept and reflect the viewpoint of school-based staff which no longer provides them with a basis for a critical look at their organisation. The best relationship is probably that of the 'critical friend'.

To summarise: the immediate implications for advisory teachers are that:

- there is a need for explicit training in the change agency role
- ways of measuring effectiveness need to be improved through developing contracting systems for interventions in schools in addition to improving the means of evaluating other areas of their work
- they need opportunities to work collaboratively with other advisory staff and should be deployed as part of a general team
- they need opportunities to develop close links with schools so as to localise their work rather than having to cover a great number of institutions at the same time

What all this amounts to from the LEAs point of view is a need to look at far more complex models for developing whole school approaches than they have tended to adopt until now. The models need to take account of a greater variety of factors and to be based upon a more open and integrated approach to in-school/out-school development. The primary functions that probably need to be performed by external agencies are those of organising and facilitating better systems of communication, increasing levels of participation and involvement and mobilising resources to target areas of development. Within the communication function, outside agencies have the means to decrease the isolation of schools and their staff and to provide a basis for schools to stand back from their own particularity and view themselves from a wider standpoint.

Turning to my own particular field, the kind of approach I am advocating requires a high level of investment in school-based development. Such an investment could be justified more easily to colleagues if it could be shown to benefit a wider range of pupils than simply those experiencing learning difficulties. The evidence from the school effectiveness movement (Mortimore et al 1988, Smith and Tomlinson 1989) provides exactly such a justification. Research reports suggest that the best way to improve provision for the generality of pupils, including those with special educational needs, is to improve the effectiveness of schools (Reynolds in ed. Ramasut 1989). Effective schools enhance learning outcomes for all their pupils.

The integration of special educational needs personnel and purposes into the whole of the advisory and support service is urgent. The new bias is for the education system to become market-led and hence, in all likelihood, more segregationist and elitist despite the introduction of an entitlement curriculum. Most advisory and support services working developmentally with schools may well face only a few years grace before they are disbanded. Those remaining in the field will have to depend almost entirely on their ability to sell themselves to the schools as the monies available to LEAs are cut to such a point that centralised funding ceases to be viable. The prognosis for the continued development of 'mainstreaming' over the next decade is not good and the task may well be to defend what has already been achieved and preserve what we can for more favourable circumstances in the future.

References

Argyris, C. (1970) *Intervention Theory and Method*. Reading Mass, Addison-Wesley Publishing Co.

Argyris, C. and Schon, D. (1980) "What is an organisation that it may learn?" in eds. Lockett & Spear, *Organisations as Systems* Milton Keynes, Open University Press.

Bass, B. M. (1984) *Stodgill's Handbook of Leadership*. London, The Free Press, Collier MacMillan.

Beckhard, R. and Harris, R. T. (1987) *Organisational Transitions*. 2nd Edition, Reading, Mass., Addison–Wesley Publishing Company.

Bennis, W. G., Benne, K. U., Chin, R., Corey, K. E. eds., (1976) *The Planning of Change*. New York, Holt Reinhart and Winston.

Biddle, B. J. and Thomas, E. J. eds., (1966) *Role Theory: Concepts and Research*. New York, Wiley and Sons Inc.

Blake, R. R. and Mouton, J. S. (1974) "Strategies of Consultation", in Bennis et al, *The Planning of Change*. New York, Holt Rinehart and Winston.

Bolam, R. (1984) Local Education Authority Advisers: Their role and future, in ed. Harling, *New Directions in Educational Leadership*. London and Philadelphia, The Falmer Press.

Bolam, R., Smith, G., Canter, H. (1978) *LEA Advisers and the Mechanisms of Innovation*. NFER Publishing Co.

Department of Education and Science (1989) *Local Management of Schools: Development Planning for Governors and Senior Managers*. London: HMSO.

Fullan, M. (1982) *The Meaning of Educational Change*. New York, Teachers College Press.

Fullan, M. (1986) "Improving the implementation of educational change", *School Organisation*. **6**, 3, pp. 321–326.

Handy, C. (1985) *Understanding Organisations*. 3rd Edition, London, Penguin.

Hargreaves, D. H. (1982) *The Challenge for the Comprehensive School: Culture, Curriculum and Community*. London, Routledge & Kegan Paul.

Joyce, B. and Showers, B. K. (1982) "The Coaching of Teaching", *Educational Leadership,* **40**, 1, pp. 4–10.'

Joyce, B. and Showers, B. K. (1988) *Student Achievement through Staff Development*. New York, Longman.

Kahn, R. L. et al in eds. Biddle and Thomas (1966) *Role Theory: Concepts and Research*. New York, Wiley and Sons Inc.

Kloska, T. (1989) Institutional Change – A Whole School Approach, in Ramasut, *A Whole School Approach to Special Needs*. London & Philadelphia: Falmer Press.

Lewin, K. (19548) *Resolving Social Conflict*. New York, Harper & Bros.

Lockett, M. and Spear, R. (1980) *Organisations as Systems*. Milton Keynes, Open University Press.

Miles, B. M., Saxl, E. R., Lieberman, A. (1988) 'What skills do educational "change agents" need? An empirical view' *Curriculum Inquiry,* **18**, 2, pp. 157–193.

Mortimore, P., Sammons, P., Stoll, L., Lewis, D., Ecob, R. (1988) *School Matters*. Exeter, Open Books.

Mulford, W. (1982) "Consulting with Education Systems is about the Facilitation of Coordinated Effort", in ed. Gray, *The Management of Educational Institutions*. Lewes: Falmer Press.

Murgatroyd, S. and Reynolds, D. (1984) The Creative Consultant: The potential use of consultancy as a method of teacher evaluation, *School Organisation*. **4**, 4, pp. 321–335.

Perls, F., Hefferline, R. F., Goodman, P. (1951) *Gestalt Therapy: Excitement and Growth in the Human Personality*. London, Souvenir Press.

Ramasut, A. ed. (1989) *Whole School Approaches to Special Needs*, London and Philadelphia, The Falmer Press.

Reeves, C. J. (1990) *Implementing Change in Special Educational Needs: the Advisory Teacher's Role in Secondary Schools*. Unpublished M.Phil thesis UEA.

Reynolds, D. (1989) "Effective Schooling for Children with Special Educational Needs: Research and its Implications", in ed. Ramasut, *Whole School Approaches to Special Needs*. London and Philadelphia, The Falmer Press.

Schein, E. H. (1969) *Process Consultation: its role in organisation development*. Reading Mass., Addison–Wesley.

Schein, E. H. and Bennis, W. G. (1965) *Personal and Organisational Change through Group Methods*. New York, Wiley.

Smith, J. and Tomlinson, S. (1989) *The School Effect*. Oxford, Policy Studies Institute.

Smith, P. (1980) *Small Groups and Personal Change*. London, Methuen.

Winkley, D. (1985) *Diplomats and Detectives: LEA advisers at work*. London, Robert Royce.

CHAPTER 3

The collaborative dimension
Risks and rewards of collaboration

Susan Hart

> "Well, in *our* country," said Alice, still panting a little, "you'd
> generally get to somewhere else – if you ran very fast for a long time, as
> we've been doing."
> "A slow sort of country!" said the Queen. "Now, *here*, you see, it
> takes all the running *you* can do to keep in the same place. If you want
> to get somewhere else, you must run at least twice as fast as that!"
> *Through the Looking Glass*, Lewis Carroll

Teachers moving into advisory or support work find themselves in
unfamiliar territory where more than previous successful experience of
teaching is needed to meet the demands which they face. This chapter
is about the difficulties of working with colleagues, and how we can
handle these in such a way as to make the best possible use of the
opportunities for enhancing classroom practice which collaborative
work provides. The central theme is that working collaboratively will
always present some difficulties, no matter how sensitively teachers
conduct their professional relationships, because these difficulties are
related to essential features of the collaborative process. What we need
to do, then, is to develop our understanding of these and other
difficulties which can arise and seek to improve our professional skills
in managing them constructively.

This central theme is of general relevance to any situations where
teachers decide, or need, to coordinate their work in teaching the same
group of pupils. It has a particular significance, however, for teachers
in advisory and support roles for whom working with colleagues is

integral (rather than peripheral) to their main professional responsibilities. The success of their contribution to the work of teachers and schools is dependent – at least in part – upon the expertise which they are able to bring to managing the collaborative process. This chapter attempts to unravel some of the complexities of this task and draw out the implications for the development of effective collaborative work.

The discussion looks in detail at one particular context: the experience of teachers in local authority support services whose function is to help schools meet 'special educational needs'. It looks critically at the models of 'good practice' presented by HMI in their most recent survey of support service work (DES, 1989) which ignore the complexities of collaborative working, contrasting these with the findings of a small-scale research project in which I became involved when working as a support teacher. This project provided an opportunity to come to terms with the difficulties which my colleagues and I were encountering in attempting to develop our work on increasingly collaborative lines. Although the outcomes of the project relate specifically to the context of special needs support, the issues raised also have wider implications and may contribute to the development of more generalised understanding of the processes and challenges of collaborative working.

The impact of the 'collaborative dimension'

At the time when I joined the project, I was working for a literacy support team which was one of many local authority support services which had been reorganised following the Warnock Report and the 1981 Education Act. Our overall brief had changed from a traditional 'remedial' style of provision to a more curriculum-focused approach concerned with helping schools 'to adapt their curriculum and teaching to better meet the needs of individual learners' (DES, ibid. 1989). This change in approach offered many advantages in principle. It created opportunities for improved curriculum access for particular children experiencing difficulties, and allowed teachers to share ideas and support one another in enhancing learning experiences for all children. In practice, there were many limitations. There was always a chronic shortage of time for discussion and planning since this was not built into existing timetabling arrangements, and everyone had so many other commitments pressing for attention in lunchtimes and after school. There was also a complex web of interpersonal and professional issues which had to be negotiated with considerable care and delicacy as part of our day to day collaborative encounters with teachers. I found that because of the tensions which these generated, working collaboratively could often seem to have an inhibiting rather than enhancing influence upon our efforts to provide worthwhile learning experiences for children.

The impact of this 'collaborative dimension' of the new support role has become a familiar topic in discussions amongst support teachers over the past few years. It is surprising, therefore, that it should have received no mention amongst the 'factors associated with success' in the most recent HMI report of support service work (DES, ibid. 1989). Admittedly, the report draws attention to many other important features, particularly in the organisation and management of support services which undoubtedly do impinge on the effectiveness of the work (see Figure 3.1). What is missing, however, is any acknowledgement that there may be difficulties associated with the new role's expectation that teachers will coordinate their work in assessing, planning for and teaching the same group of pupils.

> At best there was good cooperative work, soundly based on assessment of pupils' needs, progressive scaling of the support teachers' involvement, and a sharing with the class teacher of different teaching roles (DES, ibid. para.25).

Factors associated with 'effective support work' according to the survey include:

- a coherent LEA policy regarding role and organisation of support services
- aims of support work clearly established and negotiated with schools
- in-service provision made to support staff during period of reorganisation
- naming of support services and perceptions of role by schools and advisory services
- status and pay of support staff commensurate with role definition
- adequate time allowed in working week for production of resources
- adequate teaching resources and reprographic facilities
- classroom support worked out cooperatively, based on assessment of children's needs and linked to actual curriculum demands
- withdrawal work designed to complement curriculum work
- adequate record-keeping and liaison between teaching and support staff

Figure 3.1 Points from DES (1989) Report by HMI on a survey of support services for special educational needs (carried out between 1986–88)

The report appears to be of the view that all that is needed for teachers to work effectively together is a professional attitude and clarity of aims with regard to the purposes of their collaborative work. While support teachers have moved on, amending earlier naive assumptions (Hart, 1986) in the light of experience, the report apparently still adheres to a view of support work which takes the collaborative dimension for granted. Examples of 'good practice' are presented and commended which would be positively suicidal to attempt in all except the most exceptional circumstances:

> The support teacher worked as the second teacher for most aspects of the unit . . . making careful observations throughout. The observations recorded the difficulties experienced by some pupils as a result of the teaching system, teaching pace, classroom resources and assignments employed. Some analysis was also made of the conceptual and linguistic demands of the unit of work. The analysis was then used to determine the future involvement of the support teacher (para.26).

The example provides a perfect illustration of how the collaborative dimension of support work sets limits to what can realistically be attempted by two teachers at a particular stage of their collaborative partnership. Any support teacher would know intuitively whether it was possible, with a particular teacher, to attempt work of this high-risk nature. If the relationship was not ready, it would not be good practice but folly to attempt a style of working which virtually amounts to inviting one teacher to make an elaborate critique of the other's teaching. Whatever the fine professional intentions, sensibilities are easily exposed. Extreme caution is needed in order to raise *any* issues which might be construed as implying criticism of a colleague's work. What the report sees no reason to include is what we most need to know: how the two teachers reached the point where their partnership was sufficiently strong to be able to embark on such an approach with confidence *and* to cope with the complex feelings involved.

There is a further complication, however, which again the report fails to acknowledge. What happens if the two teachers who are supposed to be working together differ significantly in their ideas, attitudes or teaching approaches?

> The support teacher . . . worked with individual pupils or small groups to establish more precisely the exact nature of their needs. This diagnosis led to the development of a list of activities which the support teacher could provide to reduce the class teacher's burden and help to meet the need of particular pupils (para.27).

The report seems to take it for granted that teachers will be able to agree upon what children's 'needs' are and what kinds of classroom activities are needed to meet them. But what if the 'list of activities' produced by the support teacher does not fit the class teacher's perception of the problem or particular style of working? Even more awkwardly, what happens if either or both of the teachers privately disagree with (or disapprove of) aspects of one another's practice? Is it possible to achieve 'good cooperative work' when two teachers have different educational ideas, philosophies and teaching styles?

Support teachers have to be able to establish effective working relationships with any teacher in any situation. Not to acknowledge the very real difficulties which this can present is unhelpful because it sets up unrealistic expectations of what can be achieved, leading to dissatisfaction (and indeed stress) when practice always falls short of these ideals. It also delays the development of shared understandings which will enable us to prevent, resolve or work with them effectively.

I knew from my colleagues on the support team that we all faced similar difficulties and were voicing similar concerns. It seemed to me, on the basis of these first few years' experience, that the success (and, therefore, the future) of collaborative support would depend upon whether we were able to resolve the problems associated with the collaborative dimension of our developing role. What most urgently needed to be done was to bring the issues out in the open, so that they could be acknowledged and addressed. We needed to draw on our collective experience to enhance our understanding of the difficulties we were encountering and clarify the nature of the expertise required to manage them constructively. The research project described in the remainder of this chapter set out to contribute to this task.

Background to the study

A previous survey of support service work had carried out some case studies of individual teachers' work (Gross and Gipps, 1987), but ours was the first sustained, in-depth study of the development of collaborative support partnerships. We set out to look at how the presence of the support teacher was being used to create learning opportunities for children and their teachers in different situations, different classrooms, different schools and different LEAs. We wanted to document the kinds of difficulties which were encountered, how these were tackled and how the work of the partnerships developed over time. Over a period of eighteen months, we followed the work of four support teachers with eight class teachers in four different schools. We looked at the work they were undertaking from both teachers' perspectives, attempting to relate these to the classroom activities and processes occasioned by their collaboration.

The project was carried out with the cooperation of two LEAs offering contrasting models of support service work. In one of the authorities, we had access to the work of two support teachers who were members of the team offering peripatetic support to children with statements in mainstream primary schools. Their brief was clearly defined in terms of direct teaching of individual pupils, but with an advisory/consultative dimension which included offering advice about strategies and materials, joint agreement of objectives, joint planning of programmes of work and joint review of progress in agreed areas. In the other authority, access was provided to two support teachers who were members of my own team. They worked full-time for two terms in a particular school, with a brief which was open to negotiation with the head and teachers involved. Both sets of teachers had considerable experience of both mainstream and support teaching, and were regarded by their service coordinators as highly effective in their work.

Negotiating a collaborative partnership

Studying these teachers' work helped to clarify two distinct categories of 'difficulties' associated with collaborative work: those which arise from the circumstances and characteristics of *particular* partnerships, and those which are common to *all* collaborative partnerships, whatever their specific circumstances. The nature of each of these, and the skills which support teachers used to manage them effectively will be explored in turn.

Setting structures and boundaries for collaborative work

In view of the concerns with which I had embarked on the study, what struck me first about the partnerships observed was how *successful* they all managed to be (even where there were significant differences between teachers). In all cases without exception, teachers claimed to be at least reasonably comfortable with the pattern of support adopted and felt the support teacher's contribution to be worthwhile. No doubt the teachers were inclined to present their collaboration to me, as an outsider, in its most favourable light. Nevertheless, there was no doubting the genuine and spontaneous enthusiasm which a number of class teachers expressed with regard to the benefits which they felt they and the children had gained from the support teacher's presence. In one case, the support teacher was even seen as a 'life saver', turning the tide for a particular teacher and helping her to regain a more positive approach to her professional situation.

For my own part, I could not help but be impressed by the sheer variety of forms of support emerging under the auspices of the new role, and the ingenuity with which different partnerships discovered opportunities for constructive collaborative work, whatever the limitations of their respective situations. The evidence had the effect of renewing my conviction about the significant opportunities for teachers and children which collaborative work can open up, even within the constraints identified.

So what was it which accounted for their 'success'? The variety of approaches used by support teachers with different teachers (and with the same teacher over a period of time) suggested that there was no single recipe or blueprint of 'good practice' which guided their work. Support teachers did not insist upon particular preferred methods of working. What they did, it seemed, was to select from a repertoire of possible strategies those which were best suited to the needs, possibilities and constraints of a particular situation. Each pattern of support was individually constructed. Through a careful process of negotiation and decision-making (sometimes implicit, sometimes explicit), support teachers set up boundaries for their collaborative work which accommodated differences and minimised difficulties such that the two teachers were able to work constructively together whatever the circumstances and whatever the stage of their developing partnership.

This *flexibility*, it seemed, was the key. The difficulties associated with a particular partnership did not impinge upon the effectiveness of the work because a pattern of support was constructed *taking them into account*. Some examples will help to illustrate this process in particular cases, highlighting the key features of individual partnerships which led to the various forms of support adopted.

The early stages of a relationship in a new school

> The support teacher worked on a separate table with a group of six children specially identified by the class teacher as needing concentrated individual attention. The children were making their own

*books about owls (relating to the class topic on animals), work which
had been specifically planned and prepared by the support teacher, and
was different from the activities the rest of the class were engaged in.*

The support teacher was at the stage of generally establishing
relationships and feeling her way around in a new school. She felt that
it was in everyone's interests, including her own, to adopt a 'low
profile' approach. She negotiated a style of working with which she
felt very comfortable, which she knew would be very successful with
children and which would help establish her credibility. It was also a
solution which coincided with the class teacher's perceptions of the
children's pressing needs for additional individual attention. (The
class teacher was used to having other adults working in her classroom, so she was not worried by the support teacher's presence.)
While the two teachers built up their relationship, both retained
virtually complete autonomy, but doors were still left open for
discussion between them. The books which the children produced
could be displayed and shared with others, thus providing a bridge into
the general curriculum of the class, and opening up opportunities for
future development when relationships were more securely
established.

However, it was not always necessary to adopt this 'softly, softly'
rule in the early stages of every partnership. In situations where the
two teachers already had good staff room relationships and where the
support teacher's credibility was already established from her work
with other teachers, a wider range of options could be considered from
the outset.

Giving the class teacher control

*A Top Infant teacher was experimenting with collaborative story
writing with the children organised in mixed ability groups. He and the
support teacher worked together on a team-teaching basis, circulating
round the groups and giving help as necessary.*

In this situation, the two teachers had only been working as a
partnership for a few weeks. The support teacher's strategy was to
short-circuit many of the tensions arising within a new professional
relationship by giving the class teacher virtually complete control over
the nature and direction of their collaborative work. She was there as a
resource to support his work with his class, and went along with whatever he suggested even when, privately, she had doubts about it. The

collaborative story writing activity which lasted over three sessions was initiated entirely by the class teacher. He saw the support teacher's presence as an opportunity to experiment with ideas which perhaps he would not have risked on his own. He felt his own approach to writing was 'pretty traditional', and was inspired to try out new approaches by developments and discussions taking place amongst the staff within the school as a whole. Again the support teacher was doubtful whether the children would be able to cope, but kept her doubts to herself. In the event, both were astonished and excited by how capably the children responded and the quality of the writing which resulted. Both felt they would more readily include such approaches in the future.

Combining collaborative teaching with support for children

The support teacher worked with a small group of specially selected children on a series of activities which she had specifically designed for them but which formed part of a wider process of planning and development of resources for reading which she and the class teacher were engaged in on a collaborative basis.

Developments taking place within a school could exercise an important influence in negotiations between class teachers and support teachers about the specific focus of their work.

These two teachers were also in the early stages of developing their partnership, but their collaborative work fitted into a wider set of developments in the teaching of reading which had already been under way in the school for some time. The two teachers set out to try and combine specific support for individual children with an overall programme of development of resources for reading for the class as a whole. The support teacher certainly felt, with hindsight, that the pattern of working had been too ambitious. She felt that it had put too much pressure on the class teacher who was (willingly) spending vast amounts of time producing resources. The class teacher admitted to feeling some strain and difficulty in keeping up the momentum, but she was very committed to the work, which she recognised as contributing to her own professional development, as well as meeting the needs of her children. Nevertheless, the approach was enormously demanding and virtually impossible to sustain in the face of the day to day pressures of teaching.

Adapting to practical constraints

> *For one session weekly, the support teacher supervised the whole class for silent reading, sharing reading herself with individual pupils, while the class teacher worked with an individual boy on mathematics activities which the two teachers had planned jointly.*

This arrangement was arrived at following the difficulties which this particular boy found in adjusting to the once weekly visits of a peripatetic support teacher. Although the support teacher had a direct teaching brief to work with this particular boy, both teachers agreed that he would be better off maintaining the continuity and security of his relationship with the class teacher. The presence of the support teacher was used, therefore, to facilitate the provision by the class teacher of concentrated individual attention which would otherwise have been difficult to offer. The class teacher benefited from the opportunity to study the child's responses and needs more closely, and still had access to the support teacher's resources in order to discuss and plan future activities.

Meeting teachers' needs and accommodating differences

> *The support teacher took the whole class for an hour on a few occasions to allow the class teacher time to plan for and organise aspects of her writing work following discussions which they had had together.*

The support teacher suggested this opportunity to the class teacher, conscious that sometimes the form of 'support' which is most urgently needed is simply to relieve some of the pressure on teachers and provide *time* to think through aspects of their work. All the children could then benefit from more thoughtfully planned and organised activities. This situation also corresponded to how the support teacher felt best able to help given her unfamiliarity with the 'developmental' approach to teaching writing which her mainstream colleague was using. Although a very experienced teacher, she confessed to feeling uncertain about her capacity to support in this situation. She was very open to new ideas and interested to learn more about the class teacher's approach, but felt unable to trust her own intuitive responses to children in case what she was doing was in conflict with the methods being used. The class teacher, who was in her first year of teaching, also felt that she was experimenting and was happy to explore her ideas with someone who was interested, supportive, prepared to ask questions but not prejudge solutions. The two teachers shared ideas and discussed their uncertainties with regard to strategies for supporting the writing development 'needs' of particular children.

Frameworks for decision-making

These examples illustrate the complexity of the task which support teachers must undertake in organising and managing the process of collaborative work from the earliest stages of a developing partnership. Sometimes, as one support teacher put it, a partnership 'just clicks'. But most of the time successful collaborative partnerships are made, not born. They are the product of a careful (and continuing) process of negotiation and decision-making, setting up the boundaries which will structure and facilitate collaborative work. (Although, for ethical reasons, the examples selected have avoided those (few) situations where there were significant differences between teachers, in these situations the same principle of *adaptation* was applied, allowing the partnerships to work successfully within their own limits.)

An analysis was carried out of all the different models of support observed, and the range of decisions reflected in them mapped out as a general framework to guide decision making (see Figure 3.2). This framework should not be taken to imply that decisions are made on a once-and-for-all basis. Whether they are explicitly negotiated or tacitly agreed between the two teachers involved, collaborative work involves a continual process of renegotiating decisions previously taken in the light of changing perceptions, changing circumstances and new possibilities arising within the partnership.

Sources of stress in collaborative work

In spite of their evident success in devising workable frameworks for collaborative support, it was clear from the teachers' comments that the decision-making process itself was highly complex and uncertain. The 'difficulties' which it generated were not of a sort that could easily be resolved however well teachers know one another, however much they respect one another's beliefs and practices, and however much time available for discussion and planning. There are some difficulties, it seems, intrinsic to the collaborative process which *every* partnership has to come to terms with.

(1) Decisions about how the presence of the support teacher is to be used:
(a) decisions about the purpose of support: (what their partnership hopes to achieve), e.g.:

- direct support for children
- in-service opportunity for teacher
- curriculum review/adaptation/development
- joint problem-solving
- some combination of these

(b) decisions about the organisation of support: (how the support teacher's time is actually deployed in practice)

- *target children*: will specific children be targeted, and if so on what basis will they be selected?
- *grouping*: will any target children be taught as a group or integrated with the rest of class?
- *curricular continuity*: what will relationship be between work done by target children and on-going curriculum activities?
- *roles & responsibilities*: how will responsibilities for planning and preparation, and for organising, managing, teaching and evaluating the session be shared between the two teachers?

(c) decisions about the extent to which teaching decisions (see next section) would be negotiated collaboratively.

(2) Decisions about the nature of children's difficulties and the nature of educational experiences required to promote effective learning:

- decisions regarding the selection of particular aims and objectives for teaching
- decisions regarding the selection of particular activities and resources
- decisions regarding the selection of the mode of presentation, order, duration of activities
- decisions regarding the degree of control which the child is allowed over content, direction, pace of learning
- decisions regarding the extent and nature of interaction which the teacher engages in with children, or encourages the children to engage in with one another
- decisions regarding the use of praise, approval, extrinsic rewards
- decisions regarding the nature and extent of support to provide or pressure to apply

Figure 3.2 Analysis of patterns of decision-making

Coping with disturbance

For both groups of teachers but especially for class teachers, collaboration inevitably involves a *disturbance* to established ways of thinking and working. For support teachers, the disturbance arises from the need continually to adjust to new relationships: to rethink and remodel practice to suit particular circumstances. For class teachers, it means reviewing their teaching approaches and renegotiating relationships with their classes to incorporate the contribution of the second teacher. Talking with class teachers heightened appreciation of just how significant this disturbance can be (even when it only affects one small part of a week).

Some class teachers felt that the presence of the support teacher acted as an unnatural constraint upon the way in which they managed their relationships with their class:

> *I can't shout at them when you're here!*
>
> (Class teacher to support teacher, May 1989)

They also felt that the presence of a support teacher could create problems with the children. Children soon worked out that they could exploit the situation by playing off one teacher against the other, or spend all their time moving between the two teachers to get 'help'. Class teachers worried whether children would become confused as a result of receiving mixed messsages from two teachers. Some felt loath to relinquish control over their own children's learning to another teacher.

They knew (often from previous uncomfortable experience) that the presence of a support teacher could be undermining to their own professional equilibrium:

> *I used to hate it when she came in. She would just bring in her work, which had nothing to do with what we were doing, and do it with her group. I always felt she was being critical of me. It was worse than having no help at all.*
>
> (Reconstructed from interview with class teacher, March 1989)

Having a support teacher working with you could be 'the final straw' on top of an already intolerable burden of pressure and stress. On the other hand, if support work went well, it could provide an important safety valve, relieving pressure and helping to rebuild confidence when this was most needed. It could be a source of new stimulus and professional satisfaction. An atmosphere of shared interest and excitement was created which rubbed off on the children:

> *I like it when Miss is here. We do good things.*
>
> (6 year old, May 1989)

For class teachers, then, the issue was how much risk they were prepared to take in order to exploit the opportunities of collaborative working. Should they play safe, i.e. set boundaries for the collaboration which reduced disturbance, and kept additional work-load and stress on themselves to a minimum? Or should they take the opportunity to experiment, to share ideas, to learn together and live with the risks and disturbance that went with that?

Coping with loss of autonomy

Working collaboratively implies the need to take decisions jointly and, therefore, for both teachers to relinquish at least some control over their professional work. For class teachers, this represents only a small (if significant) annexation of the autonomy which they enjoy with their classes for the majority of the time. For support teachers, however, whose role is essentially collaborative, it represents an important loss of independent control. If boundaries for collaborative work are set in such a way that *most* of the decisions for planning and carrying out classroom activities are negotiated jointly (with the support teacher giving the class teacher as much control over the process as possible), the support teacher becomes *dependent* upon (and in a sense beholden to) colleagues for the conduct of her professional work. Not surprisingly, support teachers found this a strain at times:

> *You're always a guest in someone else's classroom. You're always on your best behaviour. You can never really relax and be yourself.*
>
> (Support teacher: May 1988)

There were moments when, in spite of being committed to developing collaborative styles of working, they yearned for their own space and group of children so that they could simply get on with teaching in their own way.

> *Sometimes I just wish we could go back to the old way of working. It was so much easier just to have yourself and the children to worry about!*
>
> (Support teacher's comment: May, 1988)

In negotiating patterns of working, therefore, support teachers had to be careful not to overlook their own needs and interests in the situation. How much autonomy should they retain over the decisions affecting their professional work? Should they keep some independent space to engage in work which was less stressful and which was an undoubted source of professional satisfaction (for example, working with selected individuals and groups)? Or should they pursue more collaborative approaches which were frequently stressful, yet which they were also committed to promoting in line with current thinking and legislation with regard to improving curriculum access for children with special needs?

Coping with a heightened awareness of uncertainty

Working collaboratively also has the effect of making teaching seem much more complicated than when teachers work on their own. This is not just because collaborative work superimposes a new set of decisions and responsibilities on to the already highly complex demands of teaching children. Nor is it simply because negotiating decisions jointly slows the process down through the need to justify and clarify bases for decision-making to one another. It is because discussing teaching decisions together generates a heightened awareness of alternative interpretations (and therefore uncertainties) which pass unnoticed in the high-speed process of decision-making which teachers routinely undertake on their own. In our study, discussing children's needs in order to decide how best to use the support teacher's presence led to a heightened awareness of how difficult it actually is to ascertain what children's 'needs' are. Whereas initially I had been concerned about how it was possible for two teachers with very different views to coordinate their work effectively, the research brought a new awareness of the extent of differences that will become apparent between *any* two teachers as they begin to explore together the bases upon which their complex judgements are made. Different minds inevitably bring different perspectives to the same set of events. Different perspectives highlight alternative interpretations, with the result that making decisions is experienced as more complex, uncertain and frequently more onerous than before.

Decisions about how to use the support teacher's resources to respond to children's needs also created a number of dilemmas. Even when support teachers in our study had a direct brief to support particular children, teachers were by no means convinced that the children's best interests would be served by providing additional individual or small group help. They were aware that this approach could be counterproductive for some children, who might react negatively to being singled out for special help. Equally, receiving individual attention could encourage a child to become *dependent* upon the presence of an adult during learning activities and assume that s/he could not cope without individual help.

Where it was felt that additional individual or small group support would be in children's best interests, teachers were still undecided about whether it should be the class teacher or the support teacher who should work with children experiencing difficulties.

> *I feel that they would benefit from E.'s expertise. But on the other hand, I'm with them most of the time, and if I have the opportunity to work with them in a small group, it will help me to teach them more effectively in general.*

(Class teacher: May, 1988)

In an attempt to find a balance between these various considerations, teachers frequently opted for a combination of different approaches, shifting between these according to the kinds of activities the children were to be engaged in.

Controlling stress through negotiation

In negotiating patterns of support, therefore, it was clear from the teachers' comments that they were not *just* being guided by the needs of the children as each of them perceived them. Recognising the stresses associated with the disturbance, loss of autonomy and heightened awareness of uncertainty which collaborative work entails, they were also giving careful consideration to their own and one another's needs and to the needs of their developing partnership. Through the process of negotiation they achieved a sort of *working consensus* (Hargreaves, 1972): a pattern of support which allowed for constructive collaborative work while regulating the degree of stress experienced by the partnership to a level which both teachers felt comfortable with. The process is a dynamic and continuing one. Partnerships maintain and develop themselves through a continual process of renegotiation of decisions previously taken in the light of experience.

From sources of stress to sources of professional learning

However, the answer to 'successful' collaborative work is not necessarily to seek to reduce the difficulties experienced by a partnership to a minimum. As may have already become obvious, on closer examination we can see that the *difficulties* which collaboration necessarily entails are what creates its unrivalled *opportunities* for professional learning. Viewed in a more positive light:

- *disturbance* can be seen as an *opportunity* to reconsider existing patterns of working and classroom relationships and construct them anew
- *loss of autonomy* can be seen as an *opportunity* to make explicit and clarify the basis for decisions which teachers take and to consider alternative approaches
- *heightened awareness of uncertainty* can be seen as an *opportunity* to pool resources and support one another in a continuing shared process of questioning and enquiry into teaching

If we minimise the difficulties intrinsic to the collaborative process, we do so at the expense of minimising the opportunities for professional learning which collaborative work presents. The task for support teachers, therefore, is to judge how much difficulty (or learning opportunity) a partnership can tolerate without being exposed to undue risk. Ironically, the partnerships which are most favourably situated seem likely to be most vulnerable to exposing themselves to risk in this way. Where teachers already know, like and respect one another and find one another's ideas stimulating, they are most likely to underestimate the stresses to which they may be exposing them-selves and one another as a result of trying to make the most of their partnership opportunities. Teaching is such a highly complex and sophisticated intellectual, social and emotional activity that it is inevitable that trying to mesh two professional minds productively should prove problematic. Exposing one's practice to the scrutiny of another (however sympathetic) or opening up taken for granted routines to re-examination can be painful and disorienting. Only so much uncertainty is tolerable as a stimulus for professional growth. The partnership must ensure that both teachers' confidence and sense of professional competence are safeguarded.

The skill, then, for the support teacher lies in finding the right balance between *safety* and *stress*, between *support* and *challenge*, between *consolidation* and *development*. Where this balance lies, for a particular partnership, depends (at least in part) on the strength of the professional relationship which the two teachers have been able to establish. Conscious of this, the support teachers in our study put much effort into winning the confidence, trust and respect of colleagues. They sought to establish relationships which were not just focused on work: chatting at break and lunchtime, sometimes going out for a drink together, or socialising in the evenings. They were also prepared to be 'a shoulder to cry on', allowing colleagues to off-load professional worries and tensions which could not be aired openly in the school.

Where the balance lies also depends on the willingness of both teachers to take risks and, by choice, to tolerate a higher level of stress in order to benefit from the stimulus and professional satisfaction which collaboration brings. Many of the teachers in our study took this view. Class teachers were prepared to take risks because they were carried along by an ethos of development in the school, or by the satisfaction and stimulus reported by colleagues working with the support teacher. What made up their minds, though, was the confidence which they themselves felt in the support teacher, whether they felt that there was something to be gained, for themselves professionally and for the children, by taking certain risks. Recognising this, support teachers worked hard to find ways of establishing their own expertise without presenting themselves as threatening and without undermining the 'equal partner' basis of their relationship.

Support teachers working to develop a successful partnership must, therefore, be continually working at two levels: constructing a pattern of working which will allow the partnership to be successful now, (within current limits) while at the same time laying the foundations now for the development of further collaborative work in the future.

Towards a new understanding of good practice

To return to the issues raised at the outset, the study has provided renewed confirmation of the value and potential of collaborative styles of support. Although the future of support services is currently uncertain as a result of LMS and changing arrangements at local authority level, the study confirms the need to preserve (and if possible extend) opportunities for teachers to work together and share responsibility for teaching the same group of pupils.

However, the study also shows that it would be counterproductive to invest scarce resources in encouraging collaborative forms of working if we do not at the same time acknowledge and address directly the complexities involved. Opportunities need to be provided for support teachers and mainstream colleagues to consider the issues *together* and work out together how to manage the processes effectively.

Much of the responsibility for developing the necessary skills and understanding must lie with those teachers for whom collaborative work is an integral feature of their professional role. Arguably, an implication of the research is that advisory and support work needs to be understood as a new *collaborative mode of professional practice* which requires a specific knowledge base, criteria for good practice and procedures for evaluation adapted to it. In mapping out the 'difficulties' of collaborative work and successful strategies for dealing with them, this chapter has made a contribution to defining the processes and expertise involved.

The work of the teachers in our study has demonstrated that there is a need for a much more sophisticated understanding of good practice than that revealed in the HMI report. It has shown that good practice cannot be identified in the abstract, but only by examining the circumstances of a particular partnership, and seeing how effectively the support teacher adapted to them. Good practice is determined not by *what* the support teacher *does* but by *how* what the support teacher does *relates to* the needs, possibilities and constraints of a particular situation.

This means that *any* support partnership, including those struggling to establish themselves in the least auspicious circumstances, may reflect good practice if the support teacher can justify decisions made in relation to the developmental possibilities available. It also means that impressive examples of collaborative practice such as those described in the HMI report are not ideals to which other practice should aspire, but rather available possibilities which may or may not be suited to the special circumstances of particular partnerships.

Although good practice cannot be defined in the abstract, three principles of good practice have emerged from our study, which might be claimed to describe *the procedures* through which effective collaborative support in particular cases is achieved:

Good practice is flexible

Support teachers do not insist upon particular strategies or approaches to support work. Rather they draw flexibly upon a whole repertoire of strategies which they adapt to suit each situation.

Good practice is self-critical

Support teachers recognise the uncertainty of the decision-making processes and, therefore, regard decisions taken as provisional. They keep their work continually under review, revisiting previous decisions taken in the light of experience and changing circumstances.

Good practice is developmental

Support teachers are concerned not simply with success now but with creating the conditions which will facilitate the further growth and development of the partnership, leading to further opportunities for professional learning engendered through collaboration.

In developing procedures for evaluation that are in keeping with this understanding of good practice, it has become clear through our study that assessing the support teacher's expertise in managing the collaborative dimension of the work needs to be central to any evaluation process. Whether evaluation is part of an accountability exercise or part of a process of reflective professional development, the question to be addressed is not 'what has been achieved?' in absolute terms, but rather 'how effectively have the opportunities for development in this particular situation been exploited?'

The process would involve support teachers in thinking back through the judgements, decisions and courses of action undertaken with respect to a particular partnership, reconsidering their consequences in the light of experience and reflecting on alternative strategies. A preliminary framework to guide this process, and based upon the analysis presented, is suggested in figure 3.3.

There is much work still to be done to extend our understanding of what is involved in working effectively with colleagues. Teachers in advisory and support roles will no doubt wish to consider how the outcomes of our project relate to *other* forms of collaborative practice which are not specifically focused upon classroom teaching. This chapter has presented an interpretation of collaboration as a process of negotiation of a developing partnership which is structured (implicitly or explicitly) by a set of decisions about how teachers will organise their collaborative work. We have paid most attention to the opportunities for professional learning and development engendered through this process. We have barely begun to explore the processes by which teaching and learning are enhanced through collaboration from *within* the particular boundaries decided upon. Advisory and support teachers have long known that facilitating professional development involves far more than simply *passing on* to colleagues knowledge and skills derived from their own successful classroom practice. The nature of the *processes of interaction* through which new understandings and skills are developed, and the conditions for professional learning needed to support them, are important areas for further investigation.

> 'If everybody minded their own business,' the Duchess said in a hoarse growl, 'the world would go round a deal faster than it does.'
> 'Which would *not* be an advantage,' said Alice...
>
> Lewis Carroll

A preliminary framework for evaluation

Stage 1: *How were the support teacher's resources used and why?*

(a) What steps did the support teacher take from the outset to get the relationship off to a good start? What dilemmas did this present?
(b) In negotiating patterns of working, which decisions were:
  ● explicitly negotiated between the two teachers?
  ● thought through privately by the support teacher?
  ● taken for granted?
(c) What conflicts of interest/dilemmas did the support teacher face in arriving at this pattern of working?
  ● with regard to the children's needs and interests?
  ● with regard to her own and the class teacher's needs and interests?
  ● with regard to the needs of their partnership?
  ● with regard to the practical constraints affecting the work?
  ● in attempting to reconcile all these aspects of the situation?
(d) What developmental opportunities were created, and how are these reflected in the pattern of working adopted?

Stage 2: *How did the partnership develop and what did it achieve?*

(a) What changes in patterns of working occurred or were renegotiated and what led to the changes?
(b) What steps did the support teacher take specifically to foster the development of the partnership?
(c) What difficulties arose, how did they relate to earlier patterns of decision-making, and how were they addressed?
(d) What evidence is there of the outcomes of the work? How do these relate to the teachers' original intentions? How have they been affected by factors associated with the collaborative process?

Stage 3: *With the benefit of hindsight, what alternatives might there have been?*

(a) What alternative patterns of working might have been equally well or better adapted to the needs of the situation?
(b) What alternative interpretations of the needs of the situation might there have been?
(c) What developmental opportunities were present but were not pursued?
(d) What strategies might the support teacher have adopted to open up further developmental opportunities?

Figure 3.3 Negotiating a collaborative mode of working

References

DES (1989) *A Survey of Support Services for Special Educational Needs, Report by HM Inspectors*, London: HMSO.
Gross, H. and Gipps, C. (1987) *Supporting Warnock's Eighteen Percent: Six Case Studies*, London: Falmer.
Hargreaves, D. (1972) *Interpersonal Relations and Education*, London: Routledge and Kegan Paul.
Hart, S. (1986) Evaluating Support Teaching, *Gnosis 9*, ILEA.

Acknowledgements

The research project referred to in this chapter was funded by Thames Polytechnic School of Primary Education between January 1988 and September 1989 under the directorship of Linda Harland. Our thanks are due to the schools, teachers and their LEAs who gave consent to be involved in the project, to the London Borough of Newham for continuing interest and support, and especially to Pam Corr and Eve Collis for their time, help and thoughtful comments.

CHAPTER 4

An advisory teacher – a case study

Jan Campbell

Introduction

The work of advisory teachers differs according to the Local Education Authority (LEA), and the phase or curricular area to which they are assigned. My LEA undertook substantial recruitment into the advisory service during the late 1980's, leading to an increase in the number of advisory teachers and the range of their roles and activities.

Biott (1991) comments upon the *ad hoc* way in which the role has developed in many LEA's and, in part, blames the variety of initiatives under which the jobs have been funded. These include Education Support Grants (ESG) and the Technical Vocational Educational Initiative (TVEI), amongst others.

Thus, 'advisory teacher' is a title which can be, and is, interpreted in a variety of ways, even in one authority. At the time of writing I am the sole advisory teacher for personal and social education (PSE) in an authority of 80 secondary, 9 middle, 444 primary, 31 special and 11 further education institutions (figures correct at time of writing).

My curricular area remains largely un-prescribed by national legislation yet it *must* be addressed if schools are to fulfil the requirements of Section 1 of the Education Reform Act. This places responsibility upon schools to promote 'the spiritual, moral, cultural, mental and physical development of pupils at the school and of society' and to prepare pupils 'for the opportunities, responsibilities and experiences of adult life'. (DES 1988) Thus the cross-curricular, whole staff, school-developed nature of PSE may distinguish my role from that of some other advisory teachers.

Inevitably, the nature of the curricular area flavours the illustrations upon which I draw. However, the focus of this account is not intended to be PSE, but the advisory teacher role itself. This may be viewed and defined differently by each individual or organisation involved in its provision. I examine the different perceptions, and consider if they can be compatible, or if the ambiguity creates the need for compromise. If so, I question whether this is necessarily a bad thing.

The context

My study is set in the context of one LEA at a time when an advisory service review and development process is just beginning. The process will lead to greater 'customer' orientation and improved cohesion within the service. I consider the expectations of the LEA – the prescribed/described role; the perception of some schools and my own perceptions – the perceived role; and the real profile and content of the job – the actual role.

In examining the translation of the theory of the role into the reality of work within one school, I determine the lessons learned; investigate their potential for informing other aspects of the job; and try to identify messages for others who may venture into advisory work. It is, in effect, a personal review process intended to lead to plans for increased effectiveness.

The prescribed/described role

My job description illustrates the breadth of the brief. At a County level the advisory teacher assists in the development and implementation of curricular aims and in the planning, organisation, administration and delivery of the County based in-service training (INSET) programme. To fulfil this aspect of the role, s/he needs to keep up to date with current thinking, legislation and documentation in order to contribute to the writing of local authority documents such as county policy statements and curricular guidelines.

Liaison with colleagues in the advisory service and professionals from other agencies, (especially those working for the four District Health Authorities) is fundamental to the brief, as is the management, maintenance and development of the County's collection of PSE resources.

At an area and local level, the advisory teacher offers help and advice to curriculum support groups; helps individual schools, colleges and consortia to plan curriculum developments; plans school or college-focused and consortium-focused INSET; and contributes to such INSET activities. S/he may also teach alongside class teachers in their own schools, i.e. coaching, in addition to other forms of INSET.

As a 'catch all', there may be additional duties prescribed by the responsible advisers.

The perceived role

The relative newness, and diversity of the role of advisory teacher generates inevitable confusion and uncertainty within schools. The 'advisory' aspect is associated in the minds of some with the inspectorial role of the county advisers. Robinson (1991) comments that advisory teachers 'enjoyed a certain neutrality through the exclusion of most of the more threatening inspectorial aspects of advisory work.'

Some schools want 'an expert' to explain how to approach a development: others a ready-made INSET day to solve staff training problems. One perhaps cannot blame colleagues in schools, where imposed changes come thick and fast, for trying to find a quick solution to one of the multitude of problems.

Clearly, the number of perceptions of advisory teachers is as diverse as the role itself. The advisory teacher needs to respond to the dictates of the LEA; her/his adviser; the demands of the relevant curricular area; the phase or institutional group s/he represents and - from my point of view, most importantly - the needs of the teachers to whom support is offered. Perhaps some of the misunderstandings reveal a mismatch between the way we *think* we should be working and the needs of the school! Thus the perceptions of the role by the advisory teacher may need to be examined and may also bear little resemblance to the reality of the job itself.

Holly *et al.* (1987) found, in their evaluation of the TRIST (TVEI Related In-service Training) project - the initiator of some advisory teacher posts - that several had encountered a lack of definition of their responsibilities and had had to 'learn on the hoof'. More recently Biott (1991) suggests that 'The lack of certainty about the role seems to derive less from doubts about its worth than from its transitional nature. Both the advisory teachers and the schools have been learning from trial and error.' What is needed, however, is the occasional opportunity to reflect upon the trials and to learn from both errors and achievements in order to maximise future usefulness.

The actual role

It is impossible for one person to be all things to all colleagues. In its widest interpretation, the role involves maintaining contacts in, and updating information from, not only the field of education but also beyond. One must keep school-based colleagues informed of current thinking, and seek to set it within the framework of the whole curriculum.

The school is but one part of the community, and one contributor to the education of young people. In order to work with colleagues in establishing the contribution of the school to the overall personal and social education of students, one needs to gain a whole community perspective. This in turn, is so all-embracing that only the ability to leap tall buildings and move faster than a speeding bullet could make total effectiveness possible! The focus must be, therefore, the curricular experiences of students, with the whole community as a context, rather than a brief.

The complexity of the role can seem daunting but there are many people with complementary briefs. These include those representing different curricular areas, other LEAs, and agencies outside the LEA, who are willing to form networks to share information and support. Bell (1990) defines such networks as 'point of professional communication linked by means of a social network for social improvements.' Such contact helps to put the role of the school into the community perspective; to inform others of LEA thinking, and vice versa; and to create a consistent message for young people. It can also inform colleagues of activities or experiences which they may not encounter first hand. 'Networking in this sense implies communication and partnership with a view to disseminating ideas about 'good', i.e tested practice' (Bell 1990).

Constant work with people with a different focus, or priorities can, however, lead to role conflict. Most people are, by nature, territorial, and want their priorities to be the prime beneficiary of the network. The unwary can find their needs 'hijacked' in the interests of others. I state this not as a reason for remaining in isolation but in order to make a case for standing back occasionally to re-focus and check that one's own needs are being met. Bell (1990) points out that where the knowledge gathered through networking is put into practice, gaps between partners in a network become minimal. Thus it may be possible to check the effectiveness of networks by examining how frequently we have used knowledge gained from them.

Forming networks of colleagues from a variety of disciplines results in personal support and access to a wide range of information and skills; establishing networks of teachers is essential. Through such networks, the wealth of skill and experience gained in countless classrooms can be shared. It is not just that one advisory teacher cannot 'get round' a whole county: one advisory teacher has only one set of experiences to offer, however diverse they may be. Through teacher colleagues vicarious classroom experience can be gained. We must never lose sight of the fact that the 'bottom line' of the job is the young people and their teachers.

It is in working with teachers that the focus of the role must remain if the title Advisory Teacher is to mean anything. It has little significance 'unless the person in the role is able to give appropriate, timely and meaningful advice and support to teachers in schools'. (Biott 1991) From teachers we continue to learn, to improve the quality of suport, and in-service education in its widest sense, thus giving relevance to other aspects of the job.

Support

The dictionary provides a wealth of definitions for the word 'support', many of which make the role sound like that of a pit prop. For example 'to carry the weight of . . . ' and 'to bear or withstand pressure'. The trouble with a pit prop is, that if it is removed without being replaced by another support, the roof caves in! There is also a limit to the number of roofs which can be propped up by a single support. Perhaps a little closer to the truth is 'an appliance worn to ease the strain on an injured body structure or part'. Certainly the advisory teacher should aim to ease the – not inconsiderable – strain upon colleagues in schools. It is, however, definitions such as 'to speak in favour of', 'to give aid or courage to', 'to give approval to' which come closest to my view of support. However, I must consider if a role of validation and reassurance is enough.

A 'quick fix' solution to a problem is rarely effective in the long term. Nevertheless, where a colleague feels in need of urgent assistance it may be necessary to give immediate, short term help before long term developmental planning can take place. Sometimes the number of requests can render long term involvement impossible. Perhaps something is better than nothing, especially if accompanied by suggestions about long term planning and a promise of future support.

Biott and Smith (1988) refer to 'flying visits' to conduct impressive lessons, or staff workshops' as 'seductive', but go on to say that 'progression in learning requires longer term, reflective partnerships.' Whether to develop prolonged, in-depth involvement with a few schools, or to spread oneself thinly across many is the dilemma of those who, like me, have large numbers of schools to support.

Stanton (1990) highlights the quandary, suggesting that the targeting of schools considered most in need of support can avoid the dilution of support, but asking, 'Do you only help those who invite your assistance? If you do, are they necessarily the schools most in need?'

In the following case study, my justification for the considerable time spent in one institution – the equivalent of half a day per week for the first term and one day per month for the following two terms – is the opportunity it afforded to examine my actual role. I have been able to analyse the extent to which my prescribed and actual roles are in conflict or are complementary. I can now seek to ensure that in future involvements, the time available will be used to the maximum advantage of the school. In other words, this proved an opportunity not so much to stop the 'learning on the hoof' referred to earlier but to attempt to reflect upon it!

All INSET was school-based and involved the staff in the delivery. This is in line with the findings of Trowbridge (1986) who wrote in an article in the Times Educational Supplement that teachers 'need to be less dependent on tutor-led INSET courses and to take more responsibility for the processes of their own professional development.'

Studies such as that in East Sussex (Hewton 1988) examined school-focused staff development projects to determine the possibilities for future planning. The East Sussex project 'accepted the notion that INSET should combine internal and external expertise and resources and that schools should be responsible for identifying their own needs and planning their own programmes'.

Work with one school

The school, an 11–19 mixed comprehensive, had an existing tutorial PSE programme in years seven to ten, which was to be reviewed by a new PSE coordinator (appointed in summer 1989) in order to establish cross-curricular links. Advisory support was offered by the LEA and this afforded an opportunity for me to try out some of my own ideas in a real situation, as well as providing the new coordinator with support.

Support also came from within the school. The new coordinator was an existing member of staff, a year head, held in high regard by her colleagues and with clear support from the senior management team. Aubrey (1990) states that 'unless the change agent is in a position of formal leadership or authority, it may be difficult to effect change beyond the sub-group or sub-system of the work specialisation and responsibility and thus to influence organisational change'.

As this was a whole school review, there had to be a commitment to organisational change. Thus, the status of the coordinator was doubly important.

There was a general feeling in the school that it was time to move on, so that most staff members were committed to the review. This was a school which refuted the view that 'Innovations are instinctively treated as suspect, especially if they involve any departure from routine, or require close cooperation with colleagues.' (Hargreaves, 1978). Although this view still sometimes prevails, it is encouraging that, in my specific experience, we have moved a long way from this automatic resistance to change.

In planning the review, it was important to be aware that others in the school had different priorities and pressures and that to rush might jeopardise the opportunity for development. Not all members of even the most innovative staff will be instantly excited by a major development. As Hamblin (1989) points out 'Uncooperativeness can be justifiable in the light of past experience of innovation, as well as being symptomatic of concealed anxiety . . . '. We were fortunate that, in this case, the school had a past history of successful innovation, but a sensitive approach is always necessary.

In addition to the overall review, a stop-gap programme was produced for year eleven as we progressed – a case of the 'quick fix' solution being necessary as a temporary measure.

In the following case study, I establish the stages of the development and examine my role to discover where my involvement was most effective. To clarify this I have divided the account into twelve steps, but it is important to note that the steps were not completely separate. There were overlaps between the steps, and although it is presented here in a linear form, the process might, more accurately, be described as a spiral.

Step 1 – establishing help and support

It was important to avoid a situation whereby the coordinator was working alone in the school, so we identified a group of staff members to work with her. These colleagues would support the development, and help with its coordination from within the school, whilst I offered an external perspective. The group had a representative from each faculty.

Step 2 – identifying and clarifying concerns

The first action of the group was to establish the reasons behind the need for a review. This helped to determine future action and my role within it. The following points illustrate the key concerns of the group.

In the past, pupils' views and expectations had not been determined. Establishing pupil involvement was felt to be an important step in the development.

Of widespread concern was the fact that little coordination with the subject curriculum had resulted in the problem of content overlap. The new programme should support and be supported by the subject curriculum.

The existing programme was only effective with forms whose tutor was committed to PSE. Some teachers selected only worksheet type material, perhaps because of lack of confidence with unfamiliar teaching methods. Thus there was a need for school-based INSET, particularly in classroom methods appropriate for PSE.

There was no real vertical planning. Coordination between the years was left to chance (the fact that tutors move up through the school with their forms helped but staff turnover hindered this).

Tutors felt that they did not 'own' the materials as they had had little involvement in their production. Concern was expressed that the programme did not always meet the real needs of the pupils.

Step 3 – using current work & highlighting positive points

It was important to identify and value the positive aspects of the existing scheme and of the current situation within the school. Neither the new coordinator nor I wanted to be seen as 'new brooms'. There were many good materials in the existing programme and this was to be a *development* which would grow out of, and value, existing good practice – not a complete change.

Tutorial staff were willing to be involved in reviewing the current

PSE programme in order to increase a sense of ownership, and to gain confidence in active learning methods.

The review was compatible with the review and development priorities of the school. This ensured senior management commitment and compatibility with other development priorities. Biott (1991) comments that by means of school development plans 'schools were placing themselves in a stronger position to seek specific help and to benefit from the availability of external support'.

An existing cross-curricular committee provided a communication channel for keeping everyone informed of progress, even when not all staff were directly involved with the development.

A meeting of the heads of year had already examined the existing programme and had produced six theme headings with which to work. These formed the starting point for the whole staff development. Whilst using themes as a starting point may not always be appropriate, these had grown out of, and valued, existing work, and provided a focus for staff thinking.

Step 4 – involving all staff in determining pupil needs

In order to involve *all* staff at as many stages as possible it was necessary to work within severe time constraints. The first whole staff involvement was one hour on an INSET day – not ideal but better than nothing! My job was to design and deliver an INSET session which would base the whole development upon pupil needs. It was practical and task orientated.

The information and material produced was collated, and circulated to all staff, and a replica wall chart was on the staffroom wall by the next day. This was intended to maintain momentum and interest before the pressures of the term eclipsed it! Colleagues were invited to validate, amend and add to the lists following more leisurly consideration.

Step 5 – involving pupils and investigating their views

The views of the pupils had to be incorporated since we had based the work on our view of their needs. Accordingly, pupils' opinions were canvassed. This survey was carried out by form tutors, except where they felt unable or unwilling to hold relevant discussions in which case they were conducted by the PSE coordinator.

This step proved to be one of the most important ones because as well as providing information it made pupils feel involved in the process. Most of them had clear ideas about what should, and what should not, be included in the PSE programme. For example a year nine group stressed 'not friendship *again*', but wanted instead to examine gender issues and name calling. Many groups had other comments to make about such issues as classroom organisation and pupil/teacher interaction which had implications for methodology and resourcing.

These ideas and comments were added to the information already gathered and were also disseminated to other working groups as they proved valuable not only as a contribution to the PSE review but also to other aspects of school life.

Step 6 – identifying the contribution of subject departments

I helped to organise a second session involving all staff, this time contributing to, rather than running, the event. During a one and a half hour meeting, the staff worked in subject of faculty groups to record their subject's contribution to each theme, for each year, from seven to eleven. Each group was asked to indicate, where possible, content, methodology and resources.

After the meeting the considerable amount of information was collated. In this situation, my job was to provide an extra pair of hands and to undertake the task of collating. It proved to be a valuable experience for me, since I learned a great deal about the ways in which the subject curriculum can contribute to PSE.

The questions about contributions had been open ended; the interpretation left to the groups. Had we circulated a tick list, comprising our views of areas of possible contribution and cooperation, I believe we should have missed many opportunities.

Step 7 – dissemination

Meetings were arranged to share the information gathered. The coordinator and I discussed the methods of dissemination but I was not involved in the actual process. It is interesting to note that, on reflection, I felt left out! This prompts me to ask the question 'whose needs are being met?' Is it possible that sometimes I continue involvement with a school out of personal need to see what happens, to hold on to some of the ownership? I intend to keep this in mind in future work. If members of the advisory service have support needs of their own, it is not the job of schools to meet them!

Heads of year and then year teams held meetings to discuss the information. Topics covered in the subject curriculum were examined more closely to see if all pupil needs were being met. Any needs not being met through the subjects would form the basis for the new tutorial programme. In the light of the discussions the teams identified their strengths and their INSET needs.

Step 8 – staff conference

A residential conference, part of the school's review and development programme, examined issues such as access to the curriculum and communication with parents. Half a day was devoted to methodology (one of the needs identified by year teams). Six workshops led by advisory and school staff, illustrated different classroom approaches.

Bell (1990) states: 'A central problem in the management of educational change is how teachers can gain controlled access to each other's knowledge and experience.' We found that the workshops represented one way this can be achieved; another was through classroom observation. The conference had been preceded by a two week period of classroom observation of, and by, colleagues. Teachers decided whom and what they would like to observe and made their own arrangements and negotiations. The exercise was voluntary and all but four teachers elected to take part.

The conference was extremely successful. It was well planned and delivered – by the teachers for the teachers. Advisory staff were invited to contribute to specific areas. The workshops led by teachers were just as successful as those delivered by advisory staff. This led me to consider whether my role as INSET provider is necessary in schools, or whether a contribution at the planning stage would often be enough. If I need to deliver INSET in order to develop my own skills I must be honest about it instead of pretending that it is because I have some sort of special expertise. Where teachers claim to lack expertise, it may only be confidence which is lacking. That might be enhanced by sharing the lead-in sessions with them.

Step 9 – planning vertically (across year groups)

Initially, it was intended to establish working parties to plan tutorial topics vertically, noting links with the subject curriculum. Year teams (themselves cross-curricular) were to have carried out the 'subtraction sum' between the pupil needs and the contributions of the subject curriculum, to determine the proposed content of the tutorial programme to be planned theme by theme, vertically, to ensure progression from year to year.

In fact, most of this work was carried out by the coordinator and me in order to ease the workload of the year teams. This was a time to be realistic about the viability of involving all staff at all stages. Overloading people in the name of ownership is likely to jeopardise the results already achieved.

The PSE coordinator clarified with subject teams their contributions, and discussed areas needing liaison – the subject review had revealed areas of overlap, and the need for cooperation.

Step 10 – a PSE theme inspection

The school was one of ten in the county chosen for an advisory service inspection. As an advisory teacher, I have no inspection role and neither the selection of schools, nor the inspection itself, involved me.

The inspection proved to be an unforseen positive factor! It is not one which can be built into every major development but it was vital in this one and provided an important lesson for me. The inspection facilitated the transfer of ownership of the development from me to the coordinator. Until the inspection much of the long term vision had been mine.

Unconsciously, I was allowing my enthusiasm, and desire to see what happens next, to take over. I assumed that because the work was school-based, involved all staff, and the coordinator and I worked side by side, this guaranteed ownership by the school. This was not so.

With the prospect of an inspection, the coordinator needed to prepare a presentation for the inspecting adviser. In the course of the preparation she reviewed the rationale behind the development, and determined her own plans for the future. By the end of the inspection she was leading the development, and I was truly supporting.

Step 11 – planning the tutorial programme

The year teams then met to develop the programme. Taking the results of the vertical planning exercise, with suggested topics for each year, they laid out the programme for the first term. An initial bank of recommended resources was provided, and the detailed planning and liaison work was divided up to minimise the workload for individuals, whilst keeping ownership within the team.

Step 12 – identifying further support and training needs

The staff conference provided a starting point for meeting training needs. At the end of term each team also identified areas within which they would like support, help and training. This is being built into future plans. As previously, the work supports, and is supported by, the school's review and development priorities for the year.

Needs will be reviewed at the end of the autumn term when the first term's work can be evaluated, and the next stage planned, in the light of the evaluation.

Lessons learned

The following diagram (Figure 4.1) illustrates in a simplistic linear form, my role in the various stages. This was not a case of an advisory teacher donating expertise to a school, or even working within the organisation to manage change. I was a learner, privileged to 'join in'. I could stand back from the school situation and offer an external perspective. I offered support, encouragement and a much-needed extra pair of hands. However, change must be managed from within organisations, by members of the organisation. The outsider needs to stay in the background as much as possible.

Returning to the definitions of support: taking on a 'weight bearing' support role may only lead to the eventual collapse of the development, i.e. when the external support is removed; to 'speak in favour of' and to 'give approval to' is, I believe, the true role. In this case my real role was that of validation and reassurance – not the management of the change itself.

A report of advisory teacher involvement in a school described in Brandes and Ginnis (1990) expressed surprise at 'the degree of trust that almost all of the senior colleagues placed in us so quickly. We presented all of our points as observations, not as judgements, and committed ourselves to support the school, and not to abandon them to carry out the tasks without us.' I learned from experience that whilst the staff trusted me to support them, they were happy to carry out many tasks without me, and it was important for *them* to abandon *me*.

Bell (1990) highlights the purpose of collaboration as 'the strengthening of links between partners in the enterprise of teaching' but the links between school and outsider must not be so strong that they create unhelpful dependency on either side. Through a prolonged

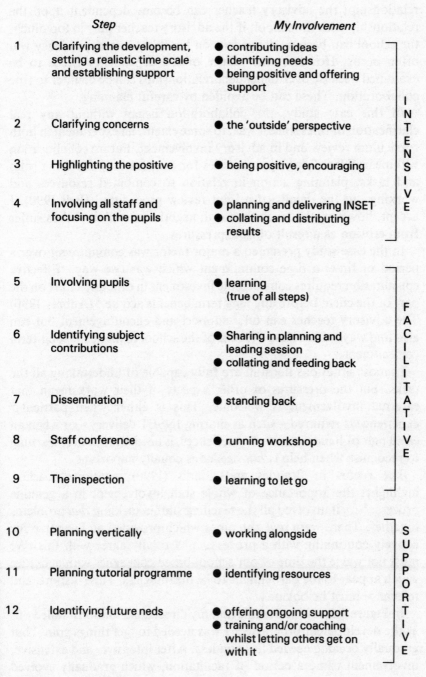

	Step	*My Involvement*	
1	Clarifying the development, setting a realistic time scale and establishing support	● contributing ideas ● identifying needs ● being positive and offering support	I N T E N S I V E
2	Clarifying concerns	● the 'outside' perspective	
3	Highlighting the positive	● being positive, encouraging	
4	Involving all staff and focusing on the pupils	● planning and delivering INSET ● collating and distributing results	
5	Involving pupils	● learning (true of all steps)	F A C I L I T A T I V E
6	Identifying subject contributions	● Sharing in planning and leading session ● collating and feeding back	
7	Dissemination	● standing back	
8	Staff conference	● running workshop	
9	The inspection	● learning to let go	
10	Planning vertically	● working alongside	S U P P O R T I V E
11	Planning tutorial programme	● identifying resources	
12	Identifying future neds	● offering ongoing support ● training and/or coaching whilst letting others get on with it	

Figure 4.1   The advisory role

relationship, the advisory teacher can become dependent upon the relationship with the school; if the advisory teacher puts in too much, the school can become dependent on her/him. Interdependency will often occur. However, the nature of the dependency needs to be examined because over-dependent relationships can be counter to true collaboration. These can be avoided by careful planning.

In this case study, the collaboration began without any real clarification of roles since it was, to some extent, an experiment in both curriculum review and in advisory involvement. Future collaboration will mean 'identifying opportunities for cooperation, clarifying roles and tasks, planning action in relation to combined resources and working out the details of a joint review procedure.' (Bell 1990). I accept, however, that such thorough negotiation will doubtless suffer from erosion as a result of time pressures.

In the case study presented a major factor was commitment over a period of time: a time commitment which was two-way. 'Effective consultation requires considerable investment in time and effort on the part of the client before any long term benefits accrue.' (Aubrey 1990) The advisory teacher can offer support and encouragement but can also find ways of enabling the staff of the school to make the long-term commitment.

In most situations the staff are fully capable of undertaking all the tasks, but the pressures of other aspects of their work mean that external involvement is welcome. This is either when particular experience is required – such as sharing INSET delivery – or when an extra pair of hands, or set of experiences, is needed. However learning to recognise when help is *not* needed is equally important.

The report in Brandes and Ginnis (1990) mentioned earlier, highlights the importance of whole staff involvement in a genuine process. ' . . . it involved all the teaching staff in tackling *real* problems together. There were *real* outcomes which provided an incentive for actively continuing with a process . . . ' I totally agree with this. We must not waste the time of our school-based colleagues with activities which appear to the participants to be meaningless. Time is short, and relevance must be obvious.

In Figure 4.1, it is noticeable that my direct contributions 'tailed off' as the development progressed. I was needed to 'get things going' but gradually became needed less and less. After intensive, and extensive, involvement came a period of facilitation, which gradually evolved into support at a distance, with the promise of 'after care' where necessary. This is as it should be. Staff know that help is available in whatever form is needed, but equally they know that they can do most things themselves.

I overhead a colleague describe the advisory role as catalytic. It is true that we can often help in speeding up a reaction, without being a permanent part of it ourselves. However, as a result of the experience recounted above, I would argue that, unlike a catalyst, we do not remain unchanged at the end of the process. Involvement with school developments offers the advisory teacher enormous scope for learning from personal experiences and from those of others. We can then go to take part in other 'reactions', but we carry with us our learning from previous ones.

A final point regarding prolonged involvement with a single institution is that I found my whole-county focus became less clear after a time. As a biologist, it is easy to become fascinated by one cell but I acknowledge that it is necessary to step back regularly to regain a view of the whole organism if the microcosmic learning is to have continued relevance.

The effects of E.R.A.

Even if long-term commitment is less extensive and intensive, the duration of involvement is important if advisory teachers or other outsiders are to play a part in organisational change. The need for an investment of time over a considerable period has already been noted (Brandes and Ginnis 1990) and Aubrey 1990. Until now schools have received this long term commitment, as well as in-service training for teachers, without charge.

Whether or not the changes being wrought by the Education Reform Act (1988) will mean the end of long term collaboration remains to be seen. The future of the advisory teacher is uncertain. Sir David Hancock, Permanent Secretary to the DES suggests that an increasing inspectorial role will increase significantly the workload of advisers. (McBride 1989) This may mean that they will have to shed the responsibility for INSET delivery. This should, he suggests, be handed over to advisory teachers. He said that 'that importance of and the need for advisory teachers during this great time of change could not be more emphasised.' (McBride ibid).

Who will pay for this if not clear. Certainly, there will be not shortage of INSET providers. Under LMS (local management for schools) schools holding the purse strings will be bombarded by people only too willing to make those 'flying visits' to conduct the impressive lessons and staff workshops condemned by Biott and Smith (1988) as 'seductive'. Brown (1989) comments on the emergence of an enterprise economy in INSET provision: 'Inset providers are exploring alternative markets for their skills, although the line between the entrepreneur and the charlatan is one which individuals make for themselves.'

It is to be hoped that LEAs will still be able to provide core services of people dedicated to true support, and prepared to provide the after care to events, which help to maximise their impact. If this service is not available to schools, the eventual losers may be the pupils.

My own LEA's advisory service review and development programme will seek ways which will enable advisory teachers to work within a more cohesive structure which supports the individual and seeks to meet the needs of schools in the most effective way possible. Thus, as long as government policies permit the LEA to provide advisory staff to support schools, the structure will be in place to improve customer service.

Conclusion

It was a luxury to study a development in detail; to feel part of an organisation; perhaps something that teachers miss when taking on an out of school role. However, to undertake such a project more than occasionally would discriminate against the maintenance of support across the whole county.

Whilst one must question the extent to which issues raised by a single involvement can be widely applied, the time taken to reflect upon the experience has been well spent. It has informed my practice by clarifying areas where over-involvement can inhibit teacher development and take up time which could be used elsewhere. Long-term commitment is important but it need not always be intensive. I have learned a number of lessons that I can apply in the future:

- being clear about whose needs are being met
- being clear about what can be offered in terms of skills and time commitment
- accepting that colleagues in schools have skills which need encouraging not replacing
- letting the teachers decide what help or advice is needed – it is their development
- stepping back when not needed

- being prepared to learn, about the development, about people, about myself
- realising that it is impossible to see everything through to the end
- remembering that the outsider is only one factor in the management of change, not the manager

By being clear about his/her own role; by negotiating with schools about the help needed; and by acting as often as possible as an *enabler*, rather than a *provider*, the advisory teacher can bring closer together the perceived and actual roles. Increased personal clarity about the role, combined with a more structured approach within the advisory service of this LEA, will close the gap between the prescribed, perceived and actual roles of the advisory teacher.

References

Aubrey, C. (1990) *Consultancy in the United Kingdom*. Lewes: Falmer Press.

Bell, G.H. (1990) Collaborative Consultancy Through Action Inquiry in Aubrey (ed) *Consultancy in the United Kingdom*. Lewes: Falmer Press.

Biott, C. (1991) *Semi-Detached Teachers: Building Support & Advisory Relationships in Classrooms*. Lewes: Falmer Press.

Biott, C. and Smith, D. (1988) *It's Early Days Yet: Towards Building Effective Support Teacher Roles*. Sunderland LEA

Brandes, D. and Ginnis, P. (1990) *The Student Centred School*. Oxford: Blackwell.

Brown, G. (1989) The Changing Face of Inset: a view from a University Department in McBride, R. *The In-Service Training of Teachers*. Lewis: Falmer Press.

Hamblin, D. (1989) *Staff Development for Pastoral Care*. Oxford: Blackwell.

Hargreaves, D.H. (1978) What Teaching Does to Teachers. New Society, 9.3.78.

Hewton, E. (1988) *School Focussed Staff Development*. Lewes: Falmer Press.

Holly, P., James, T. and Young, J. (1987) *Delta Project – The Experiences of TRIST* London: M.S.C.

McBride, R. (1989) *The In-Service Training of Teachers*. Lewes: Falmer Press.

NCC (1990) *Curriculum Guidance 3: The Whole Curriculum*. York: NCC.

Robinson, G. (1991) Advisory Teacher Management – Towards an Entitlement Model in Biott *Semi Detached Teachers* Lewes: Falmer Press.

Stanton, M. (1990) So You're an Advisory Teacher Are You? *British Journal of In Service Education* 16.1. pp. 53–58.

Trowbridge, N. (1986) 'Self-Service' *TES* 16.5.86.

CHAPTER 5

Working with and through others: aspects of communication

Colleen McLaughlin

Success of the many tasks the adviser will have to undertake will depend largely on the ability to work with and through other people. The ability to work with people is a foundation stone for school or curriculum development. In this chapter I will explore the issues involved, the necessary skills and elements of working with individuals and groups. There are other elements which the adviser needs to understand and these are discussed in the chapters by David Hopkins and others. However, the ability to understand and deal with communication is a necessary precondition for work in schools which involves teacher and school development. Before I go on to look at the nature of interpersonal skills, I will explore aspects of the adviser's work and the values, attitudes and principles which inform that work.

Most advisers arrive in post as a result of their classroom or managerial experience. Often they have expertise in an area of the curriculum or a new initiative. (England 1988) The nature of advisory work, for example, the tasks of supporting colleagues, bringing about a new development, or providing INSET, all require that the work is done through and with other people. Often little training is provided for this new way of working and advisers are expected to pick it up 'on the job'. The NFER study (Harland 1990) showed that entry into the work could be much improved.

> an absence of any clear brief of their tasks, a lack of shared information and even fairly basic physical requirements (e.g. desks)

were not properly organised – or at least information about them was not property adequately communicated.

(2.5)

Other problems experienced related to the organisation of time and tasks, something which Martyn Rouse and I discuss in more detail in our chapter in this book. However, Harland (1990) showed that many teachers in this role had to go through a process of 'learning on the hoof, by trial and error' and he found the lack of an induction period less defensible now than in the past. (para. 3.4) The fact that many advisers were on short term contracts made induction and training for the tasks even more urgent. In the present climate of agency working and 'selling' of services, I think this is now a priority.

There are other potential sources of frustration for the new adviser. One of these lies in a fundamental difference between the work of a teacher and the work of a developer. As a teacher the interaction with the task or implementation of an idea is largely a direct one. As an adviser, one is largely dependent on another teacher or group of teachers for the completion of the development. This can be frustrating and the pressure to achieve can lead to feelings of pressure and dissatisfaction. If, in addition, the adviser also has up to one hundred schools to support (Cane 1973) then the pressure can be felt even more. Jan Campbell details these feelings very clearly in her chapter. These factors are highlighted not to depress but to show that this advisory role requires new ways of thinking, working and a reconceptualisation of measures of achievement. If the new adviser does not reconceptualise the way of working, the feelings of pressure can lead to the adoption of styles of communicating and working which can become counter productive. This is explored in more detail in the following section.

The nature of the tasks

The variety of tasks which the adviser may be called upon to fulfil can include being a research partner, a supporter, a change agent, a developer, an in-service provider, a consultant, a trouble shooter, and a listener (Stanton 1990). Harland (1990) classified the roles as such: class trainer, presenter (e.g. INSET), researcher, developer, co-ordinator and administrator. He points out that the boundaries between these roles often overlap and that most roles consist of more than one function. However, the majority necessitate working with teachers and in the area of teachers' learning for, as Stenhouse (1975) said, 'there can be no educational development without teacher development.'

If the area of work in the school is to be successful, then the adviser has to resist the temptation to hold on to the development. It has to be initiated and then handed over so that the teachers feel that the development is theirs. This requires working in a way which does not create unhelpful dependency and which takes some account of how teachers learn. Drummond (1989) has described the characteristics of successful teacher learning. She argues that teachers need to have a sense of success, a sense of control, a sense of purpose, a sense of self and a sense of support. Fullan (1990) supports this. He argues that teacher learning is central to any school development and that it has been shown to be successful when it has the following elements – a knowledge of the *technical skills* required e.g. here it would be skills of interpersonal communication; a *reflective* element i.e. the teacher gains clarity, meaning and coherence by reflecting on practice; it has an element of *inquiry* i.e. there is exploration and investigation; and finally, it is *collaborative* i.e. the teacher is able to give and receive ideas and support.

Underpinning such a way of working is a set of values, which are important in their own right as well as being pragmatic and essential to successful development. These values I have called the three Rs – respect, reality and responsibility. (McLaughlin 1989) By *respect* is intended respect for the teachers and their present way of working. Wragg (1987) has reminded us that often 'improving teachers' skills requires them to change their behaviour in some way', this is threatening and takes time. Once we intrude into the teacher's way of working we are entering a very personal domain. It is to enter into the world of feelings and professional identity. This is delicate work and requires understanding and respect. I hear much talk of 'resistance', as though teachers deliberately set out to block the work of well-intentioned advisers who are attempting some new development. It is necessary to remember that resistance is a psychologically healthy activity, for it protects us from being inundated with change. Credibility and trust have to be earned, they are not automatically given. Therefore, respect is essential. This respectful way of working sometimes flies out of the window under the pressure to achieve something. The adviser under pressure may not realise that there is a danger of deskilling the teacher through pushing ahead to get the development 'achieved'.

The second R is *reality*. The adviser who is highly skilled or knowledgeable in a particular field may have a necessarily clear vision of where s/he wishes the school or teacher to be at the end of the development. This can mean that the emphasis is placed on the future rather than the present. Much well intentioned work leads to 'helpers' railroading their colleagues. It is necessary to start with and acknowledge the present reality. Only by doing this will the issues be apparent and the teacher be able to move forward. The adviser must accept the perhaps less-than-ideal present before any work can progress.

The third R is *responsibility*. If unhelpful teacher dependency is to be avoided and if any new development is to be owned and carried foward by the teacher/s, then the way of working must be based on leaving responsibility with the teacher/s. This can be a challenging and taxing mode of working. Collegiality and collaboration are commendable concepts but they are also difficult. When someone is competent in a particular field and is working with someone who is less so, it can at times seem easier and less frustrating to do the job oneself – after all it would be quicker! In this discussion of values, the notion of difficulty and difference has been alluded to. The three Rs are also pragmatic because they are based on a concept of the work as inevitably involving difference.

Difference and difficulty

Difference and difficulty are inevitable parts of change, development, and work in schools. They are not indicators of good or bad, progress or lack of it: conflict and difference will always exist and should be viewed as a normal part of everyday working. Joint working is more demanding psychologically and organisationally. Once the opportunity for interpersonal communication and collaborative working is increased the potential for conflict is increased. Furthermore, the increase in joint working does not necessarily enhance communication unless it is handled with a knowledge of the processes, skills and anticipation of hard work. As Little (1989) says 'Bluntly put, do we have in teachers' collaborative work the creative development of well informed choices, or the mutual reinforcement of poorly informed habit?' The work needs to be carefully thought through, not just set in motion while we hope for the best. Susan Hart's chapter explores this in more depth. Underpinning many people's measures of their work is a view that success will occur only when everyone is in accord. Jennifer Nias (1987) has argued for a different view, what she calls the 'constructive use of difference'. If we can use differences and difficulties as springboards for creative work, then we will not be sitting around waiting for a consensus which will never be achieved. In addition, pressure will be reduced if conflict is not seen as something which measures 'failure'. Therefore, I will argue for a way of working which adopts a problem solving, collegial approach and which details some of the skills of such.

Effective communication

If the adviser is going to be successful in working face to face with colleagues and teachers, then effective interpersonal communication is an area that must be taken absolutely seriously. The communication skills of the advisory worker are important but so too is the ability to explore the communication that exists in the schools and groups which are being worked with.

Schmuck and Runkel (1985) describe three different types of communication and these can be helpful to distinguish. The first is *unilateral* communication. This is when one person initiates the communication and the communication ends with the listener. Examples of this sort of communication include reading a morning bulletin or making an announcement at a meeting. This information may have to be relayed to other people. Lack of resources has often meant this has been a model of in-service education.

The second sort of communication is entitled *directive* communication. The interaction is face to face but the sender aims only to have the receiver understand the communication and not to comment or respond, other than to communicate that it has been understood. This has been called 'coercive communication'. Examples of this might include ensuring at an in-service session that the teachers attending understand the government's new regulations on assessment. The third category is *transactional* or two-way communication and I shall return to this in a moment.

Both unilateral and directive communication can lead to distorted communication, for they involve two, three or four steps i.e. I tell you, you then tell someone else and so on. There is plenty of scope for changing meaning, putting one's own interpretations onto the message and so on. Allport and Postman (1945) described three processes of distorting communication that can occur – levelling, sharpening and assimilating. Levelling is the process of reducing contrasts between elements of messages. Qualifying phrases are left out and the message is brought more into line with the receiver's viewpoint. Sharpening is the opposite. Elements of the message are highlighted and others forgotten. In assimilating the receiver modifies the message so that the meaning is assimilated more into her own frame of reference. The unilateral communication described before is open to all these distortions. Rumours and myths spread in this way, since the listener or recipient of the message has no opportunity to clarify. Sometimes unilateral communication is chosen as a 'quick' form of communication: it may result in taking more time to sort out the confusions.

Directive communication can lead to distorted communication because it gives the listener no opportunity to engage with the speaker and to deal with her own concerns. I may have understood your message but disagree with it and if there is no room for my own feelings and thoughts to be dealt with, I am likely to feel resentful and to distort the message if I have to pass it on. In fact, my feelings may lead me to want to discuss it a great deal.

For these reasons, transactional or two-way communication is the best way to resolve difficult issues or misunderstandings. It will also create less misunderstandings. Two-way communication involves a process whereby each person attempts to send and receive messages accurately. It also involves an attempt to understand the impact of the message on the other in terms of feelings and response. As previously suggested, not only is it important for the adviser to have the awareness and skills of working in this way in her face to face contacts, but she may need to develop this way of communicating in the groups she works with. I shall now explore the awareness and skills necessary to establish this type of communication. I shall begin by looking at interpersonal communication and then go on to examine working with groups.

Effective impersonal communication

Working with people involves emotion and messiness. It is not a neat, linear process which one can follow through step by step without deviation. It involves the notion of interdependence and effective interpersonal communication involves acceptance of this. It is to accept that my actions will affect your response and so on. Therefore, it is necessary for the adviser to take seriously the notion of self awareness of style and mode of communication in order to know how this affects the responses of others. In the ensuing discussion of skills and elements there is a danger that it is felt that I am setting up an ideal type. There is no one, right way of communicating since we all will have our own style and our strengths.

If communication is to be effective and clear, then there must be room for clearing up misunderstandings and there must be room for negotiation. Trust is important here. Most teachers have developed a healthy scepticism of interventions from 'outside' and within organisations myths can abound about the motivation for new developments. It is important that trust and credibility are established. Trust, openness, the ability to communicate during emotion and the ability to develop the personal resources of others are all important factors in organisational development. (Schmuck and Runkel 1985). The Johari Window is a useful framework for examining the openness of communication. (Luft and Ingham 1955) This model can help to look at a personal style of communicating as well as the state of communication between individuals.

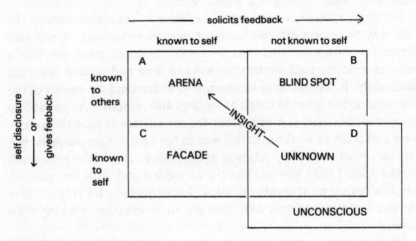

Figure 5.1   The Johari window

Square A contains a behaviour, feeling or motivation known both to oneself and others i.e. it is open and in the public arena. Square B refers to that which is known to others but not to oneself i.e. blind. Square C is that which is known to oneself but not to others i.e. it may have an element of facade which we wish to maintain. Square D is that which is unknown both to ourselves and others. There is also the additional element of the unconscious here.

According to Luft and Ingham (1955), the ideal window for effective interpersonal communication is one where the largest area is that of open communication as in Figure 5.2. Both self-awareness and open communication can be enhanced by soliciting feedback and by giving feedback or by self disclosure. By openness here is meant, 'giving

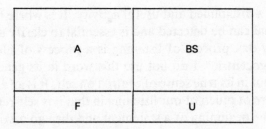

Figure 5.2. The ideal window

information that both parties need in order to get the work done or the feelings that are generated by people working together. By disclosing information that has heretofore been hidden, and by attempting to understand their blind spots, people can increase the total amount of information in the open quadrant.' (Schmuck and Runkel 1985)

To develop an open style of communication the adviser will need to develop self awareness as well as skills. The skills of effective inter-personal communication are important and can be learned, but they are set within the context of values and attitudes previously men-tioned, otherwise they become tools for manipulation. I shall now go on to explore some of these skills and ways of working.

The skills of interpersonal communication

As has already been shown, interpersonal communication is complex and open to distortion, therefore many of the skills are concerned with clarifying meaning, developing mutual understanding and working towards action in a way that is acceptable to both parties. I shall look at the skills under two main headings – working towards understanding and working on action. It is a way of working that assumes and accepts that there will be difference and conflict, there-fore, it is a way of working designed to help clarify problems and try to avoid misunderstanding.

Working towards understanding

The aim of this element of the process is to work with a colleague to develop an understanding of the issues as seen by both of you. The first and fundamental skill is that of *listening* and this, clearly, involves giving the other person time and space to talk. Listening is a highly undervalued activity and pressure to 'do' means that it is under used.

Listening is a disciplined and useful activity. It is where the issues for the individual can be detected and is essential to clarify the direction.

The every day process of listening is a process of filtering and is naturally 'egocentric'. I do not use this word in its generally perjorative sense but in its true sense of centred on self. It is an accurate label for the nature of much of our listening in that it is self-referential. We often hear the beginning of a statement and then go off onto our own track of thinking, perhaps preparing a response or attending to something about the speaker. We may not hear what is said because we are so preoccupied by our own concerns. Listening is liable to be distorted by preconceptions, prejudices and emotions. All this means that rarely do we accurately hear what is being said. For this reason, the sort of listening which is different from that just described is often called *active listening*. Active listening involves an attempt to concentrate totally on what is being said and try to receive the intended message accurately. It involves listening to the whole message i.e. the subtext as well as the spoken words. The listener needs to concentrate on three levels to what is being said. First, what is being said verbally. Are there any words which contain more power for the speaker than others? At the second level the listener is concerned with how it is being said i.e. what tone of voice is used? The third level is that of the body messages: what is being conveyed here and does it match with what is being said?

Most human beings have developed sophisticated ways of being verbally polite and of not communicating their true feelings. Body messages can be very powerful. The active listening process is a two way process, it has been compared to being similar to a radio transmission. The listener has to attend not only to the messages being received, but also to the messages being transmitted, for they will affect the incoming messages. The listener must, therefore, attend to the messages being sent out to the speaker. The three levels of communication apply here too. For example, is there consistence between the different aspects of communication? This is where the previously mentioned self awareness plays a big part. Many people send unintended messages e.g. I look at my watch because I am anxious about time and I communicate a lack of interest.

Active listening requires that the listener encourage the speaker to talk and communicate that s/he is attending by making what are known as encouraging noises. Interventions have different aims and many are aimed at checking that the communication has been accurately received or clarifying what the speaker means. Here the skills of *paraphrasing* and *reflecting back* are important. Paraphrasing involves repeating back what has been said so that it can be checked. It is not about becoming a parrot but it can help the speaker to clarify what she thinks, for it is rare that we communicate accurately first time what we mean. Reflecting back is a more sophisticated form of paraphrasing. It has many functions in addition to those already described. It communicates empathy and the sense that the other's feelings and thoughts are valued. It involves communicating or reflecting back the total message received e.g. 'You say that the last meeting went well and you are happy to go ahead as we planned, but you seem anxious about that.' Here the listener is responding to the non-verbal messages too. It is important that such mirroring statements are tentative and do not turn into amateur psycho-analysis! (A definite block to communication.)

Similarly, the feeling that one is being interrogated can hinder effective communication, therefore, the use of questions needs to be explored too as part of this first phase. *Questions* have many functions but generally people overuse them, without thinking carefully about their aim. Open questions can be helpful in expanding on what is being said e.g. 'Go on' or 'Could you tell me a bit more about that?' Questions can be used to clarify how someone feels about an issue or idea, e.g. 'Well, how do you feel about that idea?' Heron (1975) argues that as professionals we tend to avoid 'cathartic' interventions and thereby avoid an important area of communication. Feelings undiscussed will resurface in later times and may cause bigger problems than if they were allowed expression early on. Closed questions are overused and often are a way for the speaker of slipping in a statement under the guise of a question e.g. 'Do you really mean that...?' However, specific questions can be useful in focusing down on a particular issue e.g. 'You say that the meeting did not go well, but how many people showed dissatisfaction and in what way?'

This connects to another important and underestimated area, which is *an ability to deal with and communicate during emotion*. The notions of difference and difficulty have been discussed and it is during such conflicts that emotions are aroused. Ideas are owned by people and not often seen as separate from someone. My belief system is part of my identify, therefore, I may feel rejected and hurt if my ideas are 'turned down'. Similarly, in groups emotion will be aroused where there is disagreement. The adviser needs to develop an ability to communicate at times where s/he may be feeling strong emotion or where others may be feeling emotional. Clear communication may fly out of the window at such times. The skill of paraphrasing can be useful here.

A similar and important skill is that of *summarising*. Here the speaker and the listener have a chance to agree on what has been said. This is an important skill in conducting meetings too. The skills so far mentioned are all vital in working towards a common understanding. They are largely to do with opening up and expanding communication before the process of narrowing down and focusing begins. It is a fine distinction since many of the skills, such as the use of questions, can fulfil both functions. The distinction needs to be clear in the adviser's mind, i.e. the first stage of the process involves opening up communication so that issues are fully explored and then comes a stage of focusing down on specific issues and working towards action.

The process of narrowing down onto a specific focus may involve *challenging*. Since I am assuming that there will always be difference and that intentions and understandings will inevitably clash, the skills of challenging become very important. This is one of the most difficult areas of interpersonal work and it requires skill and delicacy. I would like to say first of all that it is a right that has to be earned. If one is not open to challenge oneself then one has not earned the right. Certain principles hold here. First, self-challenge is always the most successful. Second, it is always more successful to challenge from strengths rather than weaknesses. Let us abandon the myth of the perfect person who can be good at everything! A way of challenging which upholds the first principle described is to invite the other person to review the state of play e.g. 'How do you feel that it has gone so far?' or 'How do you feel we could improve the management of that?' This way of working invites the other to challenge him or herself. Challenging from strengths involves encouraging the other to use more fully an ability they have e.g. 'You say that you feel you cannot manage the meeting. I have noticed that you ran that group of pupils really well. Do you think that there are any similarities?'

This last example relates to another important skill, that of giving and receiving *feedback*. In order for feedback to be helpful it needs to be descriptive rather than judgemental; specific rather than vague; able to be acted upon; as much as the other can take rather than as much as one would like to give; and a mixture of positive and negative. Like challenging, if one is to give feedback one should expect to receive it, in fact, it is desirable to solicit it. (see the Johari Window previously mentioned.)

The final skill I wish to discuss under this first heading is that of *goal setting*. Having explored via active listening and the other skills so far described, the process often moves on to setting goals. One of the reasons so many people rarely achieve goals is that they misunderstand the difference between an aim and a goal. An aim is a statement of intent or direction, a goal is a specific framing of how to achieve the aim. A goal needs to have the following characteristics if it is to be achievable. It needs to be realistic i.e. within the bounds and capabilities of the person or group; it needs to be set within a stated time scale so that it can be reviewed; it needs to be recognisable i.e. framed in such a way that I will know when I have done it; it also needs to be sufficient to meet the aim i.e. attempts to be realistic and achievable can mean that it gets reduced so much as to be ineffective. The goal also needs to meet with ethical criteria and be acceptable to both parties. When two people can agree upon a specific and achievable goal then there is likely to be greater scope for it being accomplished.

So far I have argued that to work towards understanding and to lay a basis for action the adviser needs to be able to:

- listen actively and allow others to talk
- communicate during and deal with emotion
- paraphrase and reflect back feeling and meaning
- use questions in a constructive and varied way
- be able to open up and focus down communication
- summarise what has been said
- challenge in a helpful way and be open to challenge
- be able to give and receive feedback
- be able to work towards goal setting

Working on action

The previous section has focused on establishing what the concerns are that a colleague may have and agreeing a mutually acceptable goal or direction. This next section will look at how such goals may be translated into the reality of practice. This is an often-underemphasised part of the process. Many people feel the job is done once we have clarified what the issues are and where we want to go. The whole process can collapse unless much attention is given to the phase of action. Most people need much support in putting something into action, especially if this has been a difficult area for them in the past.

The first skill which is required is *the ability to develop strategies for action*. This is where creativity is required and developed. One is working on generating quantity of ideas and, for the moment, putting aside issues of quality or feasibility. We know that when we are under extreme pressure we tend to reduce our range of action and tend to get stuck in well tried approaches, even though they may not be effective. The colleague may, therefore, need help in seeing alternative ways of acting.

After this phase of the process, the idea or strategies need to be assessed and analysed for their practicability, therefore, the *ability to analyse the consequences* is the next skill. Under this broad heading come many different skills and qualities. It is a process of analysis, anticipation and inoculation. The strategies need to be evaluated for their acceptability, feasibility and effectiveness. The adviser needs to help the other to examine these elements and without somehow moving into a different mode i.e. becoming a teller rather than a facilitator. The ability to anticipate difficulties is central because many people feel that life will be smooth after they have planned something and, therefore, fall at the first hurdle, since they did not expect there to be any. Part of this anticipatory element involves the ability to take the standpoint of others in order to be able to consider possible problems. This is not a machiavellian process whereby if we get ahead we can out manipulate others, rather it is widening the horizon and accepting that others will have a part to play. Part of the process is involved with anticipating suports too, both personal and professional. Since most change is accompanied by anxiety, it is necessary for emotional and professional sources of support to be explored. This process of anticipating difficulties and supports can help to inoculate the colleague and develop his or her ability to act confidently. Many will know this approach under the name of a 'force field analysis'.

Having gone through these parts, the next phase is that of actually planning the action to be taken. *The ability to plan action* involves being able to turn strategies into manageable and if necessary, small steps. It is also about fostering perseverance and purposefulness, yet at the same time developing an ability to be flexible and tentative.

Finally, there is the *ability to follow up and review*. This involves elements of contracting, such as agreeing who will do what, and by when, as well agreeing how and when the review wil be done. This final element, if not done, can lead to a lot of frustration and wasted effort. To summarise then: this section has concentrated on the following elements:

- the ability to develop strategies for action
- the ability to analyse the consequences of strategies
- the ability to identify difficulties and supports
- the ability to take the standpoint of others
- the ability to plan action

- the ability to remain tentative and purposeful
- the ability to review action and follow up agreements

Working with groups

So far, I have discussed working with individuals and now I will go on to look at certain elements of working with groups. Working with groups is often more intricate than working with individuals because there are multiple interactions. However, many of the elements are similar. In order for groups to be able to function well the members need all the interpersonal abilities described in the previous section. The adviser's role may well be to teach or intervene to develop these skills. My experience is that too many assumptions are made about the readiness and ability of adults to work together in groups and that there is no groundwork laid. Since many teachers are not used to working together in this way, some preliminary work on this area will pay off greatly. Again it is important to realise that this is an area we can learn about and develop through staff development activities.

Group processes

In order to be able to work effectively with groups, we need to understand certain basic aspects of how groups work. First, it is helpful to realise that groups and their members have certain needs. They can be summarised thus: the groups need to achieve the *task*, whatever that may be; second, the members need to have their emotional needs met as they operate within the group – *the maintenance need* of the group; and lastly, individual group members will have *individual* needs. The group 'leader' has to maintain a balance between these elements in the structuring of the group and in its working, as illustrated in Figure 5.3.

Figure 5.3   Group needs

As well as meeting the individual needs of group members, the group needs to be seen as a whole too. It is important to adopt this perspective, for it has implications for proceeding e.g. all members of the group need to understand the issues and agree the decisions before the task can be said to be achieved, clearly this also meets the need for the group to maintain good relationships. One can look at certain actions which will help to facilitate achieving the task and maintaining the group emotionally.

Task focused actions

- giving information and opinions
- seeking information and opinions
- helping the group to establish direction and distributing roles
- asking questions – this facilitates understanding for all
- checking that people understand
- summarising

All these actions help the group to achieve the task. Group facilitators need to be able to use this repertoire. However, it is also necessary for group members to do the same. Some of these actions have an emotional dimension to them e.g. asking questions can sometimes be seen as a sign of weakness, it is however, very important in terms of everyone understanding the issues.

Maintenance focused actions

- checking understanding – this involves the use of previous skills such as paraphrasing
- supporting
- praising
- maintaining the energy of the group
- encouraging participation
- releasing tension – this can be though humour, however humour can also be destructive if it is sarcastic or the like
- facilitating communication between group members
- observing the processes occurring
- solving interpersonal problems

These actions can help the group to maintain good relationships and be able to complete the task in a productive and human way.

The stages groups go through

How and when these actions are used is also related to the stage of development of the group. Groups develop in discernible phases. A commonly used model can be summed up thus:

Forming – Norming – Storming – Performing – Ending (Tuckman 1965)

1. *Forming*

This is the stage when a group is coming together and is wondering about the experience. Questions such as: What is going to happen here? What will this experience be like? How will I get on with the others? How will I be treated? and How will I fit in? are uppermost in people's minds. The maintenance needs of the group are paramount at this stage and the group facilitator needs to be aware of this. The group is likely to be more dependent on the group leader at this point. The pace of work may be slower but it is important to lay the foundations here and establish a climate which meets emotional needs.

2. *Norming*

As the name suggests, the group is at this stage establishing the norms which will probably dictate the way in which group operates from now on. Issues of power and reward are current. Who will dominate? What sort of behaviour is rewarded? How are decisions made? If the group is to be effective then the group needs to take *responsibility* for its work and not be totally reliant on the group leader. Members need to be *responsive* to each other and accept their interdependence. *Co-operation* is important. *Decision making procedures* need to be clear and have an acceptable element of consensus. Finally, the group needs to be able to *confront problems*.

3. *Storming*

This is the stage which many groups try to avoid and find uncomfortable. At this stage the groups will find that there is rebellion and disagreement, 'fights' will break out. This stage has been compared to the stage of adolescence. This relates back to issues about cooperation discussed earlier in this chapter. If interaction is increased, so is the opportunity for conflict. There may well be disagreement about goals, strategies, and divergence about values. Interpersonal difficulties may arise. The group facilitator needs to withdraw from being a 'leader' and act much more as a resource to the group. This is also helpful at the stage of norming.

Other helpful things that the facilitator can do here are to help the group to see that difference is positive and can be a force for development, provide support for group members (for this will be an anxious time for many), and respond to feelings. The temptation to be authoritarian and rescue the group needs to be resisted. The skills of listening, paraphrasing and reflecting need to come to the fore.

4. Performing

Having established procedures and norms, dealt with conflict and worked together for some time, the group has reached a mature stage and should hopefully be highly productive. Often though, the group will swing from working smoothly and productively to becoming concerned with members and their personal or interpersonal concerns. The group facilitator should be prepared for these swings and for the possibility of the group returning to earlier phases. The facilitator should by now be able to delegate most functions to the group.

5. Ending

Most groups, if they have worked productively and in an emotionally satisfying way, will not want to end. Often, on INSET courses for example, groups will try to avoid ending by making elaborate arrangements to meet up again. Members may increase the conflict or the work of the group, they may exhibit anger at the group facilitator. The facilitator may help the group work through this phase by acknowledging that the group is ending and encouraging people to talk about their feelings. Reviewing the achievements and experiences of the group can be helpful.

These phases of group life apply to any groups that the adviser may be working with – working parties, INSET groups, or groups of colleagues.

Leadership

Many people still hold rather traditional or stereotypical views of leadership. A leader is felt to be the person who exhibits the most charisma and dominant behaviour. If leadership is viewed as a series of necessary and helpful actions which need to be performed in order for a group to meet the task and maintenance functions, then the way of working changes. The leader becomes more of a facilitator and resource for the group. The facilitator needs to be able to observe, analyse and intervene in group processes. S/he may also need to be able to teach and negotiate certain ways of working in order for the group to be able to work productively. In the previous section the implications of this have been alluded to. The facilitator needs to adapt her/his style to the stage of the group. Hersey and Blanchard (1977) see this process as a move along a continuum as illustrated in figure 5.4.

All of these discussions are aimed at developing an effective group or team who can work together, share feelings, communicate openly, deal with conflict and relate positively to other groups. In developing and working with these skills, advisers should above all remember that this is a human process and, therefore, it will be full of ambiguity and complexity, as well as reward.

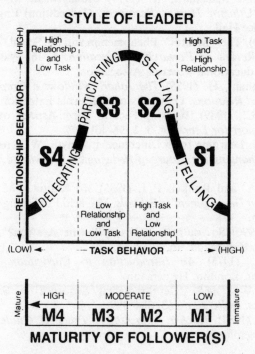

Hersey, P., & Blanchard, K. Management of Organizational Behavior: Utilizing Human Resources (3rd Edition). Englewood Cliffs, N.J.: Prentice-Hall, Inc., 1977. p. 164. Reprinted with permission.

Figure 5.4 Situational leadership

94

References

Allport, G. and Postman, L. (1945) 'The Basic Psychology of Rumor'. *Transactions of the New York Academy of Sciences (Series 2)*, **8**, 61–81.

Cane, B. (1973) 'Meeting Teachers' Needs' in Watkins, R. (1973) ed. *In-Service Training: Structure and Content*. London: Ward Lock Educational.

Drummond, M. J. (1989) 'Learning about Gender' in Lang, P. (ed) *Thinking About . . . Personal and Social Education in the Primary School*. Oxford: Blackwell.

England, J. R. (1988) 'The Role of the TRIST Consultant'. *British Journal of In-Service Education*. **14**, **2**, 117–121.

Fullan, M. (1990) 'Staff Development, Innovation, and Institutional Development' in Showers, B. (1990) *Changing School Culture Through Staff Development*. Assoc. for Supervision and Curriculum Development.

Harland, J. (1990) *The Work and Impact of Advisory Teachers*. Slough: NFER.

Heron, J. (1975) *Six Category Intervention Analysis*. Guildford: University of Surrey.

Hersey, P. and Blanchard, K. (1977) *Management of Organisational Behaviour: Utilizing Human Resources*. (3rd edition) Englewood Cliffs, N.J.: Prentice Hall.

Little, J. (1989) 'The "Mentor" Phenomenon and the Scoial Organization of Teaching'. *Review of Research in Education*. **5**, 16. Washington D.C.: American Educational Research Association.

Luft, J & Ingham, H. (1955) *The Johari Window: a Graphic Model for Interpersonal Relations*. University of California Extension Office.

McLaughlin, C., (1989) 'Working Face to Face: Aspects of Interpersonal Work.' *Support for Learning*. **3**, **2**, 96–101.

Nias, J. (1987) 'Learning from Difference' in Smyth, W. J. (ed) *Educational Teachers: Changing the Nature of Pedagogical Knowledge*. Lewes: Falmer Press.

Schmuck, R. A. and Runkel, P. J. (1985) 3rd edition. *The Handbook of Organization Development in Schools*. Mayfield Publishing Co.: Palo Alto and London.

Stanton, M. (1990) 'So You're An Advisory Teacher Are You?' *British Journal of In-Service Education*. **16**, **1**, 53–58.

Stenhouse, L. (1975) *An Introduction to Curriculum Research and Development*. London: Heinemann.

Tuckman, B. W. (1965) 'Developmental Sequence in Small Groups'. *Psychological Bulletin*, no **63**, 384–399.

Wragg, E. G. (1987) *Teacher Appraisal: a Practical Guide*. Educational: London: Macmillan.

CHAPTER 6

Managing and evaluating the work

Colleen McLaughlin and Martyn Rouse

Managing the role

A major problem facing advisory and support personnel which emerges both in the literature (Stillman and Grant 1989) and in conversations with individuals relates to the lack of clarity about the nature and purpose of the roles which they have to perform. Indeed, it could be argued that one of the greatest barrier to effectiveness, and causes of dissatisfaction with the job, arises from the lack of clear definitions and job descriptions. This is a theme introduced by Jan Campbell in her chapter in which she addresses the problems associated with the differing expectations that people have of the advisory worker. Some of these difficulties can be appreciated when one considers how the following three aspects of the role may not be congruent:

- the role as described
- the role as perceived
- the actual role

We would like to explore these different aspects of the role further.

The role as described

Stillman and Grant (1989) report that many advisers and advisory teachers are working without job descriptions although those appointed more recently are more likely to have been provided with an outline of roles and responsibilities. When job descriptions are provided, their usefulness varies. Some are likely to be extremely specific whilst others are quite general. Indeed, many descriptions provide sufficient scope for advisers and advisory teachers to develop working practices which reflect their own priorities and interests. Whatever else appears in a job description it is likely to include that catch-all phrase 'and any other duties the chief inspector deems appropriate.' This may provide the despot with unlimited scope for being creative when delegating unpleasant tasks.

The role as perceived

Individuals may have different perspectives of the advisory workers' role. Difficulties are likely to arise when teachers and heads, LEA personnel and advisory workers themselves, have differing expectations about:

- individual roles and responsibilities
- access and availability
- types of expertise on offer

In the absence of clear communication with schools about these issues there is likely to be confusion and dissatisfaction about the services provided. Ways of avoiding this confusion are considered later in this chapter.

The actual role

If there are differences between people's perceptions of the role and the actual role being performed, problems may arise. The gap between what people think the advisory worker should be doing and what they are actually doing can be narrowed by effective communication and marketing strategies. Where the gap exists, not only will there be difficulties in managing the volume of requests, but there could be more profound problems arising from the nature of the requests.

Many advisory teachers with whom we have worked report difficulties in managing the role. Given that they often have to respond to multiple managers (their senior adviser or the head of the school?) and multiple agendas (the LEA's policy or the school's needs?), it is clear that they have to take an active part in managing their own roles. In order to do the job effectively decisions have to be taken regarding:

- managing time and selecting priorities
- managing meetings

- managing boundaries
- communicating effectively
- evaluating the role
- marketing the service

Many of these topics are recurring themes in this book, but there are certain issues we should like to stress at this point.

Managing time

> There was once an old sailor my grandfather knew
> Who had so many things he wanted to do
> That whenever he thought it was time to begin
> He couldn't because of the state he was in.
>
> A. A. Milne

An advisory teacher tells a story of how during her first week in post she received no telephone calls or requests to work with schools. Her first call after eight days in post was greeted with joy. One year later she was complaining that the job was impossible as there was just too much to do and so little time. Many advisers and advisory teachers have responsibility for hundreds of schools, see for example Jan Campbell's chapter. It is impossible to respond to all schools equally. Choices have to be made if we are to avoid running round like headless chickens. How then can the workload be managed? The following points may be useful in considering what can be done:

- organise administration and report writing
- plan the day and the week
- make best use of committed time (e.g. travelling)
- identify short, medium and long term goals
- develop a sense of how long things will take
- manage meetings – always publicise finish as well as starting times
- publish times when people can see you
- make use of technical aids e.g. micro tape-recorders, answerphones
- leave time free (for reading, thinking, talking to colleagues)
- arrange for a colleague to 'rescue' you from difficult meetings
- find time to read a book on time management, for example
    Adair, J. (1987) *How to Manage Your Time* Talbot Adair.
    Austin, B. (1986) *Making Effective Use of Executive Time.*
    Management Update.
    Richardson, N. (1989) *Use of Time* Industrial Society
- learn to say no
- delegate when possible

Managing delegation

- analyse the job – what can be delegated?
- define the tasks clearly to be delegated and tell the person to whom you are delegating what is expected of them
- ensure that you delegate to those who already have, or can acquire, the appropriate skills
- use delegation to enrich the jobs of others – control, check, support and have faith
- do not use your valuable time typing with two fingers. Convince those who allocate such support that secretarial time is cheaper than your time.

Managing meetings

One of the simplest and most rewarding ways of improving productivity and job satisfaction is by improving decision making processes in the workplace. In advisory services and schools a considerable amount of time is spent in meetings. Although we hear colleagues speaking of improvements in the way meetings are now run as a result of more people attending management courses, there is still room for improvement. Most people still see meetings as a waste of valuable time which could be used doing something really useful.

There is not the time to go into detail here about how meetings can be improved. Readers will find a vast literature on this topic, particularly if one looks into the management training literature. Useful starting points would be one (of the many) books by John Adair, or Schmuck and Runkel (1985). Better still, arrange to borrow (or buy) the excellent training videos by John Cleese *Meetings Bloody Meetings* and *More Bloody Meetings*. Both are produced by Video Arts and are full of practical ideas as well as being extremely amusing.

It is also worth exploring the process of decision making within the institutions in which you are working. There are usually considerable differences between the formal (agreed) and informal (real) routes to making decisions. Who are the people with power and influence? As an outsider what do you need to know about the organisation and how it works? Time spent on getting to know the situation is usually time well spent.

Marketing the service

We do not have the space to explore all the issues involved in marketing in depth. However, it is impossible to consider the role of advisory workers without addressing some of these issues.

There can be few consequences of recent legislation which have caused greater alarm than the prospect of advisory services having to operate in the market place. The future of these services and the job security of those who work within them is in jeopardy. Commerce has come to the temple. That which was once 'free', a 'good thing' to be distributed by 'caring' LEAs is now a commodity, a service to be traded. These changes are uncomfortable and many people have reservations about self-promotion and selling themselves and their service. The language of the market place seems unfamiliar, perhaps even threatening and inconsistent with the values and aspiration of most who work in education. Are we to have 'customers', 'products', 'pricing structures', 'promotion' and 'marketing'? Are such concepts consistent with learning, growth and development? Although these changes may seem strange, there is little doubt that many advisory services have been 'producer' led, and at times the needs of the 'customers' have been ignored. There are schools which have questioned the value of much of the support they have received in the past. Others have been suspicious of the growing numbers of teachers who escaped from classroom life to a job which included pub lunches and a generous car mileage allowance.

In the (not too distant) future when a school may be able to choose between the purchase of a new set of textbooks or a day of advisory teacher's time, it is clear that support services will have to provide value for time and money if they want to survive. One consequence of this may be to force services into working in ways which feel uncomfortable or are contrary to local or national policies. It will be essential therefore for advisory services to establish a clear sense of purpose and identity which will have to be communicated to schools effectively. Schools will need to know about the range of services on offer, this entails a major marketing initiative to ensure that potential customers know what they can expect and what it will cost. If such a process seems strange then it is useful to be reminded that Handy and Aitken (1986) suggested that within the education market, four processes seem to be occurring:

- traditional client groups are changing
- traditional customers have new needs
- there are new customers
- values affecting the way people are education are changing   (p. 104)

Many LEA advisory services have in the past been characterised by producer domination, a condition in which consumers (schools) are expected to be grateful for being given the chance to avail themselves of the services on offer. Bowles (1989) points out that this sort of posture is likely to be found where there is scarcity of supply, or the product is unique, or no competition exists because there is a monopoly supplier.

Competition between services now exists. LEA boundaries are no longer the barrier they once were; different services may be fishing in the same pond. Because schools are free to buy from where ever they wish, the need to develop a marketing strategy is crucial. McCarthy (cited in Bowles 1989) explored the crucial relationship between consumer demand, product planning, selling and market research. He formulated what is known as the four Ps:

- Product
- Price
- Promotion
- Place

It may be useful for advisory services to consider their marketing strategies in the light of McCarthy's four P's:

- What is our product? What skills do we have? What are we prepared to do? What do schools want?
- What will it cost? What commitment will we require from teachers and schools?
- How shall we communicate? Do we advertise? Do we wait for requests or solicit business?
- Where will we work? In schools? At our base? What about ambience, comfort, catering?

Evaluation of the work

Before considering the details of evaluating advisory work, it is necessary to explore some models and think about evaluation. Recent experiences in in-service education have shown that there are certain traps into which we can fall. Evaluation can be seen as end point activity which is based upon a consumer satisfaction model. This model is based upon the notion that the service is delivered and then the consumers are asked whether they were 'happy' with what they received. At the outset of training days a few years ago, we were asked to deliver a session and then we were graded on a scale of one to five by the participants. Apart from the personal discomfort, there were many issues raised. Aims were not taken into account and they may not have included making the participants 'happy'; the effectiveness of the in-service work would be hard to evaluate instantly; and there were many factors which may have effected the context. Therefore, we need to move on towards a model of evaluation which acknowledges the full complexity of the work and at the same time is able to explore the impact of the work done.

The approach which follows is based upon certain key ideas. First, that evaluation is not an end point activity but is a process which is built into all stages of the work. Second, that it needs to be thought through and the criteria made explicit early on in the process of intervention. Third, that it should provide useful feedback to the adviser and the school or institution involved. Last is the concept that there are many interrelated factors which will affect the impact of the work. All these need to be taken into consideration if the locus of evaluation and decision making is to be sited in the correct place.

The Chinese Box Model of the work

There are many factors which will affect the impact of the work of the adviser. The work which takes place within the school does not occur in a vacuum. Actions and decisions which take place at different levels will affect significantly what happens in the school. The adviser needs

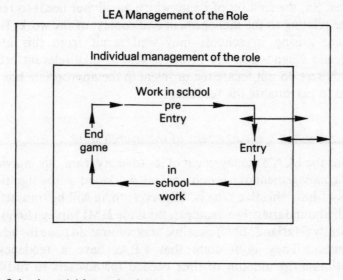

Figure 6.1 A model for evaluation

to be able to locate the appropriate area for evaluation and decision making, as hard as this may be. Figure 6.1 demonstrates the concept. The work can, therefore be evaluated and reviewed at all these levels.

1. LEA management of the role

The management of the advisory service by the LEA has been shown to be significant in the effectiveness of advisory work. HMI in their survey of support services for special educational needs (1989) detailed many factors at this level. The clarity of the brief of the adviser was affected by whether there was a clear, communicated policy and pattern of working. Where there was such a policy, which included clear aims and objectives, advisers were able to work with direction and to a shared rationale. HMI found that the ability to achieve aims varied and where the advisory service shared common goals there was less conflict in the schools. Where there was a lack of shared goals, advisers often encountered conflict over their perceived role and schools often received conflicting recommendations. One of their conclusions was that 'only a few LEAs provide clear and co-ordinated leadership for their services.' (para. 48. 1989. HMI)

Harland (1990) also found that managerial issues affected the impact of advisory work. His study identified the 'effective management and organization of the advisory teacher teams', as well as 'continuity in advisory teacher staffing policies' (p. 48) as key factors affecting outcomes. So, the first set of issues which an adviser needs to review are those relating to the management and context of the work. Issues which are arising in schools may well result from this arena. Appropriate diagnosis is key in being able to take relevant action. Many advisers do not locate the problem in the appropriate box and can tend to personalise the feedback.

2. The individual's management of the overall work

As well as the LEA's management of its advisory team, the individual adviser's management of her or his overall workload will be significant in terms of how effective s/he is. However, there will be transactions across the boundaries. For example, both the HMI survey (1989) and NFER study (Harland, 1990) cite time allocation as an issue for adviser effectiveness. They both state that LEAs have a tendency to underestimate the amount of time needed for advisers to fulfil the describe role. So time management, which is an issue for review and evaluation, may be properly seen as a management issue for the LEA, as well as an issue for the indivudal adviser's personal ability to manage and distribute the time in the most efficient way.

The questions and areas for review in this area of the work are to do with how the adviser manages the workload. Partly, this is dependent on a realistic view of the tasks and an understanding of the nature of advisory work e.g. if the adviser understands that change and development need to be planned and orchestrated, then sufficient time will be allocated to planning, negotiating, reviewing or following up. This will alter the way time is allocated. Harland (1990) points to certain key factors here. He cites the following as key to effective impact:

- the skills of the advisory teacher
- the length and frequency of advisory teacher inputs
- the capacity to sustain inservice support and curriculum developments
- the extent of the opportunity to talk to teachers before and after an input, especially if it involves working in the classroom

These factors are more fully explored in David Hopkins' chapter, but they are fundamental to where and how the efforts of the adviser are distributed. It will follow that the adviser is inevitably going to have to prioritise her/his efforts and that s/he will have to deal with conflicting demands, perhaps even different views of the role.

3. Work in the school

As suggested in figure 6.1 there are four potential points at which the adviser can evaluate or check. The first is to do with what happens before entry into the school or college. Harland's (1990) work identified the importance of 'the selection criteria and process by which shools are drawn into working with advisory teachers' (p. 49).

Some questions of relevance here are: How was entry negotiated? What was the intention behind this? Who in the school negotiated entry and what impact might this have? What are the perceptions of the participants regarding the visit or intervention? All of these factors can affect the impact of the work and may need openly addressing on entry to the school. For example, one adviser spent many weeks in a school working hard and well. It was not until weeks into the process that she discovered that the school had had an HMI inspection the previous term and the staff felt that the INSET work was only a sop by the headteacher, therefore they could not take it seriously. The biography of the school and its emotional climate will need to be considered in evaluating the work. The reason for taking such factors into account is not so that blame can be apportioned but so that there can be realistic placement of effort.

The second point which can be examined is that of entry to the institution and how that is handled. Harland's study (1990) discusses the helpfulness or not of contracts. '... The majority preferred that this should remain a verbal agreement rather than a formally written contract.' (p. 34) What does come through as important here is the idea of some initial or preliminary negotiation where the provider and the institution can clarify roles, perceptions and expectations. This is an important area for evaluation later on; much can depend upon the effective management of this stage of the process. HMI (1989) stated, in the conclusion to their study, that 'the services best received in schools negotiate carefully the exact nature of the support they can offer.' This applies to the level of LEA management as well as to the level of negotiating on entry to a school.

The third stage for evaluation is that of the work itself conducted in the school. This is often where most people focus their efforts and locate the issues: it is hoped from what has already been said that the balance has been redressed and that advisers will now see that many issues would be better located at another point. Certain questions raised earlier apply here too e.g. who is the best person to work with?

HMI (1989) acknowledged that 'the work done by support services takes a variety of forms'. (54) Harland's study has some helpful points here. One of the key factors in terms of the impact of the work was to 'ensure that the impact of an advisory teacher is spread and embedded across several staff.' (p. 45) This last point, like many others, will of course depend upon the aims and intentions of the work in the school and it is difficult to state generalisations because of the variety of the work. Advisers can review whether the way of working matched the most effective mode of working. Harland (1990) does highlight that need 'when planning, setting up and reviewing the progress of advisory teams, to devote sufficient time to identify the exact purposes intended for the team. Similarly, it subsequently requires a commitment to reappraise whether the elected modes of working adequately reflect the stated intentions for the particular team concerned.' (p. 29)

Harland (ibid.) identified four modes of working. These are, briefly put, the *provisionary* mode, where the adviser is operating as a provider of materials and resources. This mode was found to be effective as a mode of gaining entry to a school and was often appreciated by teachers. However, it was found that this mode, if used initially, was often hard to move away from and it did not address the fundamental question of how the materials were used by the teacher.

The second mode is entitled the *hortative* mode. Here the adviser is exhorting or encouraging the teacher/s to use certain methods, materials. The adviser is acting as advocate rather than just provider. Harland found that this sort of advice was often given in one-to-one conversations and was highly contextualised. This mode of working was not found to be effective if used on its own. If combined with other modes, it was found to be more effective.

The third mode of working was the *role modelling* mode. As the name suggests, the adviser is here acting as a demonstrator of some skill or method. 'Although the role modelling method certainly appears to be an important weapon in the total inservice armoury, the tendency for it to lead to uncritical and rather behaviouristic imitations of the demonstrated approach suggests that it could be beneficial to offer it in conjunction with other modes.' Harland (1990)

The final mode is called the *zetetic* mode. Here the adviser is acting more as a critical friend, who is encouraging the teachers to inquire reflectively into their classroom practice and the pupils' learning. It may well involve observation of the teacher. Harland (ibid.) identifies this as a high risk strategy and one which requires good interpersonal and relationship building skills. When it works it can be highly productive. It is suggested that advisers need to use a combination of all four modes.

The final stage of the process is the end game phase, where the adviser is working towards ending direct work in the school. This is often a stage of the work which does not receive sufficient attention or evaluation. Jan Campbell in her chapter has much of great value to say about this and about how difficult it can be. Some points worth mentioning here are that the adviser needs to evaluate how ready the teacher/s are to take on the work. Harland (1990) noted that the existence of self-support systems and staff discussion groups within the school was significant in how much impact the adviser had. This points to the establishment of structure and systems which will take the initiative forward. The adviser may need to evaluate how effective s/he has been in establishing these and in being able to assess the follow-up support that the school may need. The ending of work is a stage that has to be planned and orchestrated if the work is not to die with the exit of the adviser. The allocation of time to this stage of the process is important and often undervalued. This is an example of the links between the different elements in this model. Time allocated is linked to an understanding of the nature of the work.

References

Adair, J. (1987) *How to Manage Your Time*, Talbot Adair.

Austin, B. (1986) *Making Effective Use of Executive Time*. Shrewsbury Management Update.

Bowles, G. (1989) Marketing and Promotion to Fiddler, R. and Bowles, G. (eds) *Effective Local Management of Schools*. London: Longman.

DES (1989) *A Survey of Support Services for Special Educational Needs. Report by HMI* London: HMSO.

Handy, C. & Aitken, R. (1986) *Understanding Schools as Organisations*. London: Penguin.

Harland, J. (1990) *The Work and Impact of Advisory Teachers*. Windsor: NFER-Nelson.

Richardson, N. (1989) *Use of Time*. London Industrial Society.

Schmuck, R. & Runkel, P. (1985) *The Handbook of Organisation Development in Schools (3rd ed)*. Palo Alto: Mayfield Publishing.

Stillman , A. & Grant, M. (1989) *The LEA Adviser – A Changing Role*. Windsor: NFER-Nelson.

The John Cleese videos are available from Video Arts, 2nd Floor, Dunbarton House, 68 Oxford St., London W1N 9LA.

CHAPTER 7

Effective INSET: the role of the outsider

Martyn Rouse

Introduction

Many advisory personnel spend a considerable proportion of their working week in planning, delivering and evaluating INSET. Indeed it could be argued that a major function of any advisory and support service should be concerned with staff development. This chapter will consider some aspects of what is known about effective staff development by looking at a particular initiative which was designed to link the individual development of teachers with school improvement at the institutional level.

In times of rapid change within the education service, the place of INSET has become not only the subject of change in itself but also has been seen as having the power to play a central role in facilitating the changes which are seen to be required in schools. And yet, it could be argued that there is little evidence to show that traditional forms of INSET bring about significant changes in schools. The high cost of long award-bearing courses, attendance at which required teachers to leave school, together with the low levels of impact such courses made upon the educational experience of pupils, was the starting point for a new, but equally naïve view of staff development. Because it was increasingly recognised that many long courses were detached from the realities of schools and classroom life, many INSET decisions and functions were relocated to schools. This process coincided with the delegation of INSET budgets and the government's imposition of training (Baker) days in schools. The one day (compulsory) workshop may have brought staff development physically closer to the classroom but again there is little evidence to show that classroom practice improved. It could be argued that many 'Baker Days' were little more than tokenism which enabled a school's staff to claim about some aspect of school development 'Oh, we've done that'. . . . There were, and still are, many examples of so-called staff development which ignore the accumulating knowledge, much of it outlined in the rest of this book, about the conditions necessary for individual and institutional change.

We have known for some time (Joyce & Showers 1988, Rubin 1978, Wideen and Andrews 1987, Hopkins 1986) what makes effective staff development, but as Fullan (1990) states

> Despite the fact that we know a great deal about what effective staff development looks like, it is still not well practised. There are at least two major and often mutually reinforcing reasons for this. One is technical – it takes a great deal of wisdom, skill and persistance to design and carry out successful staff development activities. The other is political. Staff development is big business, as much related to power, bureaucratic positioning and territoriality as it is to helping teachers and students.

The initiative described in this chapter attempts to address some of the difficulties outlined by Fullan above. It also stresses the important role that outside supporters have to play in the development of collaborative attempts to link individual and institutional development.

Collaborative INSET

A more detailed account of this joint LEA and higher education initiative can be found elsewhere (Rouse and Balshaw 1991). Whilst the aim of the initiative was to develop whole school approaches to meeting special educational needs, the principles involved and the lessons learned are applicable to a wide range of development work in schools. The in-service training courses which followed the implementation of the 1981 Education Act were the starting point for this initiative. Over recent years a significant number of teachers have undertaken government funded, one term, full time equivalent courses in a range of national priority areas. However, the extent to which these courses brought about change was unpredictable. Local investigations and research by Hegarty and Moses (1988) discovered a number of shortcomings. Briefly these were:

- there was no organised system of selection of schools or individuals
- there was no real preparation or negotiation in schools
- there was no expectation of involvement by the headteacher or by the rest of the school in any depth
- the learning stopped with the teacher who 'did' the course. It was not effective in educating the school as a whole, as it dealt with skills rather than whole curriculum issues
- there was no system of 'aftercare' and support to sustain any changes in attitudes and practice which might have occured.
- the course took little account of local and LEA need

More recently, government imposed changes in funding for in-service education for teachers (INSET) have led to the belief that courses which involve the collaboration of schools, local education authorities (LEAs) and higher education (HE) may well be central to INSET provision during the 1990s. Individual needs and local requirements will have to be met through courses which allow for the simultaneous development of professional expertise and whole school policies which arise from school development plans (Jeffs 1987).

Underpinning the establishment of this initiative were eight principles which broadly reflected the changing trends in staff development. The initiative was clearly perceived as having three major phases which reflect the stages described by Miles (1986) as essential components of successful change projects: initiation, implementation, institutionalisation. This was an attempt to avoid some of the shortcomings detailed earlier and in order to incorporate some of the growing body of knowledge about effective staff development referred to earlier.

The eight principles

(1) *Local knowledge and collaboration* amongst all participants are positive pre-requisites to an initiative such as this.
(2) *Negotiation* should be carried out to try and ensure that school and individual needs are met.
(3) *Outside involvement and support* is to be seen as an integral part in order to meet LEA, area, local and school needs.
(4) *The course aims and ethos* need to take into account the current thinking on curriculum and school development. The aims should be differentiated to meet a variety of needs.

(5) *The structure* should allow preparation, negotiation, needs identification, practice and feedback, and support.

(6) *Whole school approaches* should be integral to the school-based development so all personnel are involved at the appropriate level.

(7) *'Ownership'* by the school of the work should be encouraged at an early stage to enhance the changes of maintaining initiatives in the follow-up phase, where 'ownership' or 'institutionalisation' can be seen as criteria for successful change.

(8) *Long-term review and support* should be built in from the early stages and maintained for a considerable period. INSET without 'aftercare' is seen as very vulnerable, so an attempt to ensure continuing development and change should exist as central to any course desing.

The course team

The course team normally consists of five people; two LEA area coordinators for special educational needs (advisers), two external support teachers (advisory teachers) who have direct involvement with the schools selected for the course and a tutor from Cambridge Institute of Education (CIE). An important feature of this initiative is the joint involvement of LEA personnel in planning, delivering and evaluation. To improve communication and commitment particular geographical areas are targeted each year. It is the support teachers who have a responsibility for these localities who then join the course team.

This arrangement facilitates the availability of information and support throughout all three phases of the course. The course is then available in different parts of the LEA in subsequent years. Consequently, there is continuity in the course team in that the tutor from CIE and the two members of the LEA advisory team do not change, whilst the two support teachers are new each year and bring fresh perspective and detailed information about their schools. This structure provides the LEA support teachers with the chance of working on a substantial INSET course under supervision and gives them numerous opportunities to consider and develop their own skills as providers of staff developments (Miles, Saxl and Lieberman 1988, Davies and Davies 1988).

Stages

There are three discernible stages to the initiative, in line with the principles outlined previously:

Phase one, the pre-course phase during which schools are invited by the LEA to review their existing policies and practice for meeting special educational need with a view to agreeing on an area for development. Although no specific process is suggested, it is hoped that the schools would go through a GRIDS type exercise (McMahon *et al.*, 1984) in order to select the topic for development within the school. This topic forms the basis of the school based project. In recent years schools have been encouraged to link the project to their school development plan, (Hargreaves *et al.*, 1989), and National Curriculum initiatives.

Phase two covers the taught part of the course. During this phase, course participants work with their colleagues on the development and implementation of their school based projects. The role of support personnel is again crucial during this phase as INSET deliverers and active supporters of the school projects.

Phase three is the post course phase during which outside support is provided for participants and their schools to enable the projects to become institutionalised. The support teachers have a vital role to play in setting up and facilitating support groups which continue to meet long after the course has finished.

Professional developments for participants

Whilst the focus of this initiative is on school development it is strongly felt that course members should benefit personally. It is necessary to point out that course members are all experienced teachers. Most of them carry the responsibility for coordinating their school's response to special educational needs. As Huberman and Miles (1984) point out, motives such as professional development and career opportunities are at least as important as the content of innovation and its possibilities for helping pupils. With this in mind credits towards the Institute's Modular Advanced Diploma in Educational Studies are awarded to those students who wish to continue to work towards further qualifications.

Evaluation

The evaluation of staff development programmes designed to bring about change in schoools is acknowledged to be complex because of the large number of variables involved. Joyce and Showers (1988) refer to variables which are interlinked and need to be considered in this way when evaluating and INSET initiative. These variables are the teachers, the institutions, the training programme and also the students or pupils. Evidence was found that in each of these sets of variables change had occurred as a result of the initiative.

Briefly, there was evidence that change had occurred:

for individual teachers in:

- their confidence and self-esteem
- their skills and self appraisal
- their ability to be open with colleagues

for schools in:

- INSET and staff development which improved teachers' skills
- INSET and staff development leading to changes in classroom practice
- the development of new 'norms' and ethos
- the types and range of support offered to pupils

for pupils in:

- curriculum provision
- types and range of support received.

There was evidence that certain aspects of course design and delivery need more careful attention. These are:

- making best possible use of local knowledge in reviewing the needs of schools
- making the submissions resulting from these negotiations assume the level of contractual commitment from all sides
- ensuring that all the local support team are involved as much as possible to guard against discontinuity through support staff changes
- making the best use of the initial day conference to determine the participants' needs and negotiate the content
- making sure that the best possible use is made of the time the head and course member spend together on the course
- attempting to build in a more reliable system of 'aftercare' at both formal and informal levels involving support personnel.

The role of the outsider

One of the major outcomes of this initiative is based upon the vital role played by the support teachers who are member of the course team. Not only have they played an important role in ensuring school development, but they have been able to develop their own skills as providers and facilitators of staff development in a supervised setting. Reviewing the part that such personnel are often called upon to play in school improvement programmes Saxl, Lieberman and Miles (1987) point out,

> These programmes often depend on special 'assisters' who act as consultants, facilitators and staff developers. However, these individuals are often new to their roles, with inadequate training and support for the complex task of supporting school change efforts

The scope for establishing collaborative INSET in the future which involves schools' support personnel and higher education may be difficult but is essential if we are to avoid a series of one-off, hit and run workshops which meet neither the needs of individuals nor the schools in which they work. The danger is, that as schools are encouraged to become more autonomous and competitive, professional development opportunities will be restricted to within the four walls of the school. The consequence of such inward looking policies would produce INSET as incest.

The outside supporter has a vital role to play not only in running staff development but also acting as a facilitator of networks and support groups. Such teams could prove vital. Cox (1983) refers to a 'constellation of assisters working with teachers... to adopt or develop, implement and institutionalise a new practice'. Whatever the future of INSET funding arrangements, there will continue to be a need for quality staff development programmes which address the needs of the individual as well as the needs of the school. Outside support has a vital role to play in ensuring that the gains made over recent years are not lost.

Conclusion

The experience of working on this initiative over a period of five years has been in the main a positive one for all concerned. There have been benfits for individuals and the change process in schools has been facilitated. In the words of Holly and Southworth (1989).

> INSET, when defined in these terms, is synonymous with staff development and, indeed, school based development itself ... and this means that INSET is fast becoming a built-in as opposed to a bolt-on operation.

> (p. 114)

The eight principles outlined above, together with the phasing of the initiative, has enabled wide involvement in the school-based projects which in turn had led to a feeling of ownership of the change within schools.

The collaborative nature in which the course team and participants have worked together has helped teachers to work in conjunction with their colleagues back in school. This seems to have instilled, through modelling, demonstration and practice a new confidence which has led to increased competence. Joyce and Showers (1988) describe it in these terms,

> Effective staff development requires cooperative relationships that break down the isolation and increase the collective strength of the community of educators who staff the school.

Rouse and Balshaw (1991) list a set of conditions which seem to be necessary for the success of such staff and school development:

- building a local knowledge of schools
- initial negotiation involving all staff of the school to identify development needs
- formulating a contract between the individual, the school, the LEA and higher education
- a taught element which stresses process as well as content
- interactive presentation
- projects which are likely to be of benefit to pupils
- active support of the headteacher
- opportunities for course members to pursue their own professional development and career opportunities
- formative evaluation across the whole programme and summative evaluation of the project as well as the course
- continued post course support for participants and their schools by the local support team

Advisory personnel have a key role to play as facilitators and staff developers, but I would suggest that the demand for improved preparation and continued support for advisory workers need to be urgently addressed. The need for a major training initiative for these people is crucial if they are to be effective in the changing roles they are expected to perform. Sadly, the privatisation of such services will mean that such training is unlikely to materialise. In this case teachers, schools and pupils will be the losers unless innovative forms of collaborative INSET can be developed as a matter of urgency.

References

Cox, P. L. (1983) Complementary Roles in Successful Change. *Educational Leadership*. Vol 41 (3).

Davies, J. and Davies, P. (1988) Developing Credibility as a Support and Advisory Teacher. *Support for Learning* Vol 3 (1).

Fullan, M. G. (1990) Staff Development, Innovation, and Institutional Development in Joyce, B. *Changing School Culture Through Staff Development*. ASCD.

Hargreaves, D. *et al.*, (1989) *Planning for School Development*. London: DES.

Hegarty, S. and Moses, D. (1988) *Developing Expertise*. Windsor: NFER-Nelson.

Holly, P. and Southworth, G. (1989) *The Developing School*. Lewes: The Falmer Press.

Hopkins, D. (Ed) (1986) *In-Service Training and Educational Development*. London: Croom Helm.

Huberman, A. and Miles, M. (1984) *Innovation Up Close*. New York: Plenum Press.

Jeffs, A. (1987) SENIOS – INSET sense in action. *Inspection and Advice*. Vol. 22, no. 2, pp. 19–22.

Joyce, B. and Showers, B. (1988) *Student Achievement through Staff Development*. New York: Longman.

McMahon A. et al (1984) *The GRIDS Handbook* (primary and secondary school versions) York: Longman for the Schools Council.

Miles, M. (1986) Research findings on the Stages of School Improvement. Paper presented at Conference on Planned Change. The Ontario Institute for Studies in Education.

Miles, M., Saxl, E. and Lieberman, A. (1988) What skills do Education 'Change Agents' Need? An Empirical View. *Curriculum Inquiry*. Vol. 18 (2).

Rouse, M. and Balshaw, M. (1991) Collaborative INSET and Special Educational Needs in Upton, G. (ed). *Staff Development for Special Educational Needs*. London: David Fulton.

Rubin, L. (1978) *The In-Service Education of Teachers, Trends, Processes and Prescriptions*. Boston MA: Allyn and Bacon.

Saxl, E., Lieberman, A. and Miles, M. (1987) Help is at hand: New knowledge for teachers as staff developers. *Journal of Staff Development* (8) 1 pp. 7–11.

Wideen, M. and Andrews, I. (1987) *Staff Development for School Improvement*. Lewes: The Falmer Press.

CHAPTER 8

Providing an advisory service to schools in the 1990s

Mel West

Introduction

Though the function of the educational adviser can be traced back over many years, the expansion in numbers of advisers following local government reorganisation and the creation of new Local Education Authorities in 1974, marked a significant new emphasis. Indeed, it can perhaps be regarded as the point from which the notion of a group of LEA-based personnel providing curriculum guidance to schools was effectively launched. The period from 1974 up to the Education Reform Act of 1988 saw significant development in the scope of and increasingly large numbers involved in this advisory service. Terminology varied between authorities (such staff were variously known as Inspectors, Advisers, Advisory teachers etc.) but by the mid-1980s LEAs had developed the service as one which both scrutinized school practice and stimulated curricular development. The delineation between these activities was not always clear, though, towards the end of this period, increasing numbers of staff performing advisory functions were specifically funded to support specific local or national curricular initiatives. Though school's contact with, and estimates of the value of such services varied greatly, since they were essentially seen as 'an extra', there was no serious lobby to reduce the levels of activity. The Reform Act, therefore, has brought with it a radical change in both the status of those local authority staff working to support schools, and (increasingly) in the attitudes of schools

116

towards such staff. The typical response of LEAs confronted by the twin pressures of devolving increasing number of functions and responsibilities to school level, whilst maintaining some mechanism for assuring 'quality control' within educational provision, seems to be leading towards a restructuring of advisory services. Most often this restructuring would seem to involve a separation between inspection and advisory functions. In this separation, inspection remains a centrally managed function of the LEA, and the major implications of this are dealt with elsewhere in this book (see chapter 9).

Those left providing curricular advice and support to schools, however, face a less certain future. This chapter considers the position of these advisory staff in the face of financial devolution, identifies some of the issues confronting those engaged in this work, and offers some suggestions on how advisory teachers can best serve schools (and thereby secure their own positions) during a period of fundamental and accelerating change within the educational system.

Finding a role

A recent Audit Commission paper *Losing an Empire. Finding a Role*: *the LEA of the Future* (1989), acknowledges that advisory services have been the main source of advice to teachers on curriculum and training needs. It questions, however, the scope of advice and support, indicating that in future, advice on financial and staffing matters, for example, will be as important as advice on curricular issues. It also points out that whereas 'advice' in the past has been given on the basis of what was accepted as constituting sound educational practice, in the future such advice will need to be tempered by an understanding of the resources available to and the priorities of the particular school. Furthermore, it predicts that in future it will be headteachers and governors who become the principal targets for such advice, rather than individual teachers.

> Authorities will need to consider the composition of their advisory teams . . . . Setting the balance between ease of contact and breadth of expertise will be difficult. The way in which LEAs resolve this point will influence their relationships with their institutions. They would do well to gain a clear understanding of the attitudes of headteachers, principals and governors to the authority and the perceptions they have of its strengths and weaknesses in the past.
>
> (Audit Commission 1989)

There would seem to be two clear implications here for those working within the advisory service. First, there is the question of 'match' between areas in which advice will be required and the range of expertise available amongst existing advisory staff. One aspect of this is the implication that subject advisers will need to give way to, or at least be supplemented by, a range of staff who can provide advice on management issues. Another is that LEAs will need to consider how far the pattern of subject expertise available matches the requirements of the National Curriculum (subjects and cross-curricular aspects) and the needs of the school population, though where staff with the new patterns of expertise required will come from remains problematic. Second, there would appear to be implications for how advisory teachers work with schools in the future, with changes necessary in relationships with both schools and teachers, and very probably changes too in patterns of work. This has major training implications for advisory staff, and also raises issues about the LEA structure in which such staff will operate.

If the Audit Commission's analysis is accurate, then there are two questions which will need to be considered immediately by those responsible for and working within the new context:

What will schools and teachers expect of advisory and support teachers in the future? How can the service be organised so that these expectations can be met?

Clarifying expectations

Though there have been enormous changes in the educational landscape, it must be remembered that in planning for the future of any organisation it is important to take account of that organisation's history. In the case of LEA advisers, the history of each service will continue to influence expectations, even as a new role is delineated. A review of recent history suggests that as the scope of advisory services has developed over the years there has been a tendency to accrete more and more functions into it without systematic review of whether the range of these functions was either appropriate or feasible. At the same time, and despite the growth in staffing levels working within this service, the total numbers involved remain small in relation to the school and teacher populations. It is easy for those who work regularly with or within the LEA, and who are in frequent contact with LEA projects and provision, to over-estimate the level of contact between members of the advisory service and teachers. Even where there has been contact between the advisory service and a particular school, it is often the case that many teachers in that school are barely aware that the adviser has 'visited'. Perhaps this low incidence of real contact explains the bewildering list of expectations teachers seem to nurture about the role of the advisory service.

Eraut has identified one such list:

- the 'Expert'
- the Resource Provider
- the Promoter (of policies, ideas)
- the Career Agent (facilitating teachers' career and promotion opportunities)
- the Link (to sources of information, advice, other schools and teachers)
- the Legitimator (or thinking and practice)
- the Process Helper
- the Counsellor (personal and professional)
- the Ideas Provider (a source of suggestions, but with no authority over or accountability for teacher actions)
- the Change Agent
- the Inspector/Evaluator

(Eraut, 1977)

Daunting as such a list is, it is conceivable that an adviser *could* fulfil all these roles at different times. However, it is likely that where a number of different teachers in a given school are working with an adviser, each will bring her/his different expectations to bear simultaneously. Multiply this by the number of schools an adviser is likely to be working with at any one time, and the pressures are obvious. There is also the issue of how appropriate such expectations are – should teachers expect advisers to be able to function as counsellors, for example, or are there potential dangers to teachers and advisers alike in such transactions?

Examining the relationship from the other side, Pearce produced a list of the main activities on which advisers spent their time:

- knowing the schools
- using the knowledge
- supporting the schools
- staff appointments and deployment
- providing advice
- working with governing bodies
- personal and professional support of teachers
- curriculum development and innovation
- curriculum guidelines

(Pearce 1986)

Familiar as the items on this list are, Pearce rather implies a coherence of purpose which is rarely apparent to the teachers who 'benefit' from advisory work. He also includes activities with which advisers should perhaps never have become involved. (What real expertise can they offer in selection matters for example?) – and underlines the differences in work patterns which emerge within this list. His explanation of the consequent lack of impact in terms of poor time management and conflicting priorities rings true, but the overwhelming impression from his researches is of a group who are unwilling to sacrifice individual autonomy even if this reduces their level of influence on schools.

These two approaches serve to illustrate the gap between thinking about advisory work and what advisers actually do, a point which is powerfully argued in NFER's study of adviser roles.

> Advisers, as a whole, do not do the same work. Beyond the planning and provision of INSET, there were no 'adviser' tasks common to all advisers. It would seem helpful for planning and communication considerations if the idea of a mythical generic adviser disappeared and comments were now targeted at work-related groups...
>
> (Stillman and Grant 1989)

The legacy is then one of unrealistic expectations from schools, poor definition and coordination of adviser roles by LEAs, and enormous variation in work patterns of advisers which have been determined, in part at least, by individual priorities, preferences and prejudices. Added to this, an increasing proportion of 'advice' has been provided in the most recent years by advisory teachers – a specifically funded group plucked out of schools to serve specific initiatives but often finding themselves drawn into general advisory functions. A further complication arises from the levels of activity themselves – whether the efforts of advisory staff have been coordinated behind agreed objectives or not, they have certainly been trying to do too much, and have accordingly been enduring high levels of pressure and work-related stress.

This is not to imply that advisory services have failed to influence schools, indeed whilst underlining the lack of time and numbers, the NFER survey referred to above found both headteachers and heads of departments generally positive about their own contacts with advisers. But satisfaction tended to be both individual and specific and was likely to be curriculum related. There was little evidence to suggest that a wider acceptance of adviser expertise has occurred and, as Heller

(1988) points out, Everard's comments on the degree to which headteachers value more general contributions from advisers has probably not changed.

> ... I note the low regard in which many heads hold their advisers when it comes to giving them useful advice on management problems . . . . The credibility of the advisory service does not stand very high, outside curriculum issues.
>
> (Everard, 1986)

There is an irony here. In developing their role of supporting schools advisers would seem to have to *expand* their range of expertise (or at least teachers' perceptions of what this expertise relates to) whilst *restricting* the range of activities in which they become involved, so that teacher expectations are correspondingly realistic. Though this could be managed at an individual level, if each adviser could clearly articulate the range of issues to which he or she can usefully contribute and communicate this accurately to schools, it would also be necessary, however, to 'agree' with each school how the relevant expertise would be fed into the school's decision-making processes. This would mean that 'negotiating' with schools would become a major activity for advisers and a further pressure on time. It is sensible, therefore, to consider whether there are patterns of organisation the LEA could adopt which will both give a clearer indication to schools of what they might expect from various groups within the advisory services, and provide a framework in which school-adviser contacts can be planned and coordinated.

Creating an organisational framework

The 1986 NFER survey of LEA advisory services indicated wide differences in structure and organisation. From this data, Stillman and Grant (1989) argued that ten distinct models could be identified, graduated according to the degree to which the principle of hierarchy could be discerned within and throughout the structure. The key variables influencing placement were outlined as: the amount of the chief adviser's time devoted to the advisory service; the presence/absence of a middle management tier within the advisory service; whether the chief adviser was a member of the senior management team within the education department.

Four other factors were used to help locate any one LEA structure within the ten 'models'; whether the LEA had adopted an area basis for operations (decentralisation was taken to imply hierarchy); the status of the advisory service within the LEA; the degree to which adviser and officer work had been integrated (and the consequent merging of advisory structures into the broader structures of the LEA); and the size of the service (the larger the service the greater the possibilities for hierarchical arrangements).

What is interesting here is not the 'spread' of the LEA structures produced by the application of this approach (which, though it leads to some interesting observations from the authors, could never be more than arbitrary) but that the variables used to describe differences in structure focus almost entirely on the relationship between the advisory service and the LEA. Whilst this is clearly one relationship which needs to be considered, many would feel that it is rather less important than the relationship between advisers and schools. In shaping an advisory service for the 1990s and beyond, we need to acknowledge that the 1988 Education Act has fundamentally altered the balance of influence within the LEA. If one side of this is that,

> The changes require a new culture and philosophy of the organisation of education at the school level
>
> (Coopers and Lybrand 1988)

then the other is surely a corresponding adjustment within the LEA, as increasingly the LEA will come under pressure to demonstrate that functions such as advice and support to schools are provided to meet the needs of schools, rather than to serve its own educational, managerial or control preferences.

Indeed, there is already evidence that LEAs are responding to this change, notably in the separation of inspection activities from advisory services – the one continuing to be centrally directed by the LEA, the other moving towards a 'market-led' approach. It should not be assumed that such a transformation will be achieved painlessly however. At minimum, restructuring is likely to create confusion and dislocation. Many schools and teachers who have valued and benefited from the advisory service may find themselves cut off from their source of advice – perhaps simultaneously acquiring a 'pastoral' inspector who may have no specific knowledge or experience of the area, the school, or the particular phase of education. Inevitably, there will be anxiety and uncertainty within the advisory service itself, as decisions about the levels and methods of funding may well mean that fewer staff will be employed. There is also the question of the best 'mix' – many existing advisory services were built up before the National

Curriculum became established as the dominant force in curricular development over the next decade, and significant re-staffing may be required if the service is going to be a realistic partner in these developments.

Working with schools

The LEA will need to be clear, therefore, about the range of advisory services to be provided, and about the mechanisms through which such services are made available to schools

> Whatever the nature of the support authorities provide to their institutions, there are also important issues to solve on the way in which it is provided. Though many LEAs will find the notion unfamiliar there may be cause for entering into contractual arrangements whereby services are provided by the centre to an agreed specification and at an agreed price.
>
> (Audit Commission 1989)

Though a range of 'delivery structures' are possible, whether advisory services are transferred to some form of contract on a 'pay-as-you-use' basis, or continue to be provided on the basis of notional allocations to schools, it will be vital to ensure that schools feel that the service represents 'value for money'. Several factors would help here:

- stating clearly what support services are available and at what cost to schools
- explaining the bases used for determining which services are to be provided and for calculating costs
- Establishing systems to
  - record the use made of services by particular schools
  - charge schools according to use
  - monitor patterns of use and review provision in the light of this

Above all, the LEA will need to enter into *dialogue* with schools about support services – if the provision of such services is to be demand-led, such services will only survive if they are seen as a direct response to the felt needs of schools. Nor should the LEA be drawn into protectionism; though it may seem attractive in the short-term to offer inducements to schools to 'buy into' LEA sponsored support, the long-term survival of the advisory service will hinge on its quality and effectiveness, not its cost to schools. Establishing how the advisory support links with other forms of external advice, development and

INSET provision is, therefore, another important aspect of the LEA's strategic role – the aim being to provide the best pattern of support for schools whatever its source, not the best level of support which can be mustered internally. We must look to LEAs to tackle this with vision and creativity, protecting by projecting what is worthwhile, being prepared to contract where LEA resources are considered inadequate or inappropriate. If they fail in this task, such is the market power of schools that it will not merely be the future of advisory services but the future role of the LEA itself which will come under threat.

There are then some major issues to be tackled in re-organising advisory services, issues which will require changes in the culture of the LEA, the cultures of advisers and advisory teachers and, ultimately, in the cultures of schools, if they are determined to make best use of external support in pursuing internal objectives. Nor will the changes in schools' attitudes and approach be the least important. Mulford (1982) has listed some of the factors which have made it difficult for 'outsiders' to influence schools:

- *Low rewards associated with cooperation* – indeed active collaboration with advisers often simply increases workload and pressure.
- *School structures tend to reinforce independence.* Despite recent developments in teaching styles there are still timetabling constraints and, frequently, low task interdependence between teachers. This reduces collaboration within schools and consequently teachers are less likely to seek collaboration with external partners.
- *Conflict avoidance* – schools have been characterised as 'conflict-avoiding' cultures, that is, places where staff would prefer to avoid exploring differences rather than accept the social and personal consequences of tackling these. Consequently developments which might precipitate conflict or controversy, such as debate about methods or approaches, are also avoided.
- *Multiple goals* – in the past schools have been organisations which nurtured multiple, and sometimes conflicting, goals amongst staff members. Indeed, there is sometimes an approach to headship which seems to rely on teachers identifying and pursuing their own goals. National Curriculum requirements and the growth of whole school development planning may engender a clearer set of common purposes in the future, though any advantages this offers to those seeking to work with schools could be offset by a tendency to 'shut out' outsiders during this phase of 'drawing together' amongst the school community

To some degree the developments of recent years (e.g. TVEI, GCSE) may have begun to break down such barriers, but it must be remembered that there are still large numbers of schools where substantial contact, let alone cooperation, with advisers or advisory teachers has not taken place. This is a difficult issue for those in support roles to tackle, since changing the cultures of schools to make them more receptive to outside influences will be a slow and time-consuming process, in which there is little which will substitute for personal contact and trust. It may be, however, that the production of 'School Development Plans', coupled with National Curriculum, demands, will create significant shifts. Certainly, it will be much more difficult in the future to pursue individual or departmental goals, and many of the challenges currently confronting schools have underlined for teachers the inter-dependence of their roles. There is even hope that teachers will see practical rewards in collaboration – at least in terms of increased understanding and hopefully in terms of developing their skills. Conflict avoidance remains a feature of school culture which is difficult to change, however, and those working in support roles will need to be wary therefore. But there is much that an outsider can contribute to conflict resolution, so advisers need to develop the skills appropriate to managing and resolving conflict, though precipitating it is still probably antithetical to the schools' notion of support – however useful.

Developing appropriate skills

Though the issues identified above indicate that the 1990s will bring enormous challenges to those engaged in helping and supporting schools, there will also be significant opportunities. Indeed the volume and pace of change means that many teachers feel disorientated, confused, perhaps even deskilled. There is a widespread acceptance that schools must change, but fewer specific ideas about what needs to be changed and how necessary changes can best be brought about. This, then, offers one starting point for thinking about how the adviser can key into the school system. Regardless of phase or subject expertise, advisers must be credible as agents of change.

Much has been written about the promotion of and support required for effective change. Fullan (1982) and Fullan and Park (1981) provide a useful theoretical framework. Bolam (1984) summarises the major research findings, and in so doing underlines the need to provide support beyond the point of implementation – a clear opportunity for those with advisory roles. Heller (1985) and Everard and Morris (1985) put forward distinctive and useful approaches, both of which are enormously helpful to those who are thinking about changing practice in schools. More recently, West and Ainscow (1991) offer some practical suggestions for 'getting started' within a school setting.

What is common to these writings and particularly important therefore to those who wish to change schools, would seem to be self-evident – a belief that change needs to be managed to be successful. What, then, seems to be involved in 'managing' change?

First, there needs to be some understanding of what management means – not self-management, or time management though both of these are important aspects of adviser effectiveness, but the broader process of 'getting things done through people.' Though there are many variations in emphasis, almost all definitions of the management role derive from the writings of Fayol and Drucker, which can be summarised thus:

- to establish objectives (organisational and personal) and to communicate these effectively
- to plan (with those involved) how objectives are to be pursued
- to organise staff and resources so that plans can be implemented
- to motivate and to develop staff so that objectives can be realised
- to monitor performance and progress

If the above list is accepted as a basis for adviser collaboration with a particular school, then it would not follow that the adviser him/herself is expected to carry out all these tasks. However, since the evidence is that the tasks do need to be carried out, it is important that the adviser is aware and makes sure that staff in the school are aware, of the need to ensure that someone or some method has been agreed for carrying out each one. Advisers can then contribute across the range of management activities, though the particular emphasis, the balance between school self-direction and adviser influence, will need to vary according to such factors as the nature of the project, the experience (or lack of it) amongst the staff and the skills of the adviser. So, though it is neither necessary nor desirable that an adviser manage a particular change on behalf of the school, it is vital that he/she is able to contribute to the management process as and when needed, and, at a more general level can stimulate the school towards a rational and managerially sound approach to change.

The degree to which a particular adviser is able to fulfil this role will of course depend upon her/his own skills and credibility with the school's staff. Here, at least four qualities would seem to be important:

i) *Relevant experience* Is the adviser someone who has experiences appropriate to the area of school life being tackled? Does s/he have a successful record of curricular development *within* a school? Is experience recent and relevant, and if not, what has the adviser done to remain in touch with the daily working lives and pressures of teachers?

(*ii*) *Appropriate values and attitudes* Is the adviser someone whose values and beliefs reflect the concerns and priorities of teachers? Is it clear that the adviser's commitment is towards improving the quality of experience the school makes available to pupils and to staff (and not to promote the 'pet projects' of the LEA)? Does the adviser understand and relate to the values (implicit and explicit) which the particular school seeks to embody in its transactions with pupils, parents, teachers etc?

(*iii*) *Relevant knowledge* Is the adviser's knowledge of subject areas, type/phase of school issue being addressed, sufficient? Clearly, given the limited number of advisers and the large number of schools, subjects etc. this could be a problematic area. What will be important will be the adviser's ability to draw on relevant knowledge when her/his own is inadequate; to locate this, both inside and outside the school, and to bring it to bear on the situation. Also useful here will be the ability to generalise from experience and to use knowledge in a range of contexts and situations in a manner which illuminates.

(*iv*) *Relevant skills* Does the adviser have the sort of skills which are needed to support the proposed development? In particular:

- does s/he have the necessary conceptual skills to envisage and to communicate the development to teachers; to fit the development into the wider context of the school and its purposes?
- does s/he possess the interpersonal skills necessary to work with staff during times of change and stress? Leading, facilitating, sharing, communicating, negotiating will all be important, as will be the ability to work through conflict.
- technical skills may also be important – particularly where the change involves some development of teaching approach or assessment. The ability to perform alongside teachers in the classroom has both practical and motivational implications. The ability to train colleagues seems to be an increasingly important aspect of the adviser role, and will also be a determinant of adviser credibility.

Whilst it is clear that many staff currently employed as advisers and advisory teachers possess these qualities, it is less clear that they know how best to deploy them in transactions with schools. In part, this probably relates to poor appreciation of the wider managerial context of advisory work than is desirable, but it is also a consequence of the lack of specific training for an advisory role in most LEAs. Typically, those who find themselves in the advisory service have been identified as successful practitioners, effective teachers who have coped with change within their own subject areas and classrooms. Beyond that little can safely be assumed, and those in advisory roles often meet with a number of difficulties which could, with planning and preparation from the LEA, have been avoided. Such difficulties include:

Lack of guidance about how to engage with schools from the outside. Many advisers find the 'school' difficult to come to terms with. Who do they need to talk to? What do they need to find out about the school's internal power and decision structures? What Pearce (1986) described as 'Knowing the Schools' is an activity which will take months in most cases, years in some. Clearly there are more and less productive ways of approaching schools, which are presently most often hit upon through intuition or 'trial and error.' It is important to identify and to disseminate instances of good practice, to produce clear guidance for advisers in those vital early months in the job and, if possible, to provide parallel guidance to schools about how to use advisory services optimally.

Lack of preparation for working with adults. However effective advisory staff may have been within the school, they will frequently have little experience of working with adults. Though this becomes most apparent in the INSET role which has increasingly fallen to advisory staff, it is an implicit part of all that they do. Recent research by John Harland underlines this – the spread of 'roles' most often undertaken by advisory teachers in his survey were very clearly teacher-related rather than pupil-related:

- classroom-focused practitioners promoting staff and curriculum development by working alongside teacher in the classroom (class trainer);
- presenter of INSET sessions and workshops;
- researcher by, for example, surveying schools' current practice in areas of management or the curriculum;
- curriculum or policy developer by, for example, fostering school involvement in systems for recording achievement;
- coordinator of teams of advisory teachers and ESG initiatives;
- central administrator for a specific task such as organising training requirements for GCSE.

(Harland 1990)

What would seem to be needed then is an induction programme for advisory staff which helps them first to recognise the differences between working with pupils and working with adults, and then the similarities – i.e. the extent to which their classroom skills are transferable in training situations.

Little experience of self/time management Schools are highly structured work environments – the discipline imposed by availability of resources, the pattern of the school day and the timetable 'relieve' individual teachers of many decisions about time and timing. Being let loose within the authority without a timetable can be liberating at first but many advisory staff experience real difficulties in making the best use of their time and their expertise. On the one hand, clear guidance on priorities, and perhaps suggested 'norms' for levels of contact and patterns of activity from the LEA would help here. On the other, some training in personal time-planning and management, including assertiveness, would seem to be a vital part of induction into advisory roles. It is much easier to develop effective time-management strategies from the beginning than to impose these, once unsatisfactory work patterns have developed.

Uncertainty about personal future

Significant numbers of advisory staff have been taken out of schools on secondment. This creates pressure on both the school and the individual – the one 'deprived' of a highly competent and, typically, irreplaceable resource, the other often ambivalent about whether an advisory post constitutes a 'reward' or a 'punishment'. As a consequence there is often instability within advisory teams, as those within the role seek something more 'permanent' and 'secure'. The most effective remedy for this would seem to be to establish as free a movement between school-based and LEA-based posts as possible but recent legislation has made this harder to do, as the LEA can no longer retain 'advisory posts' unless its stock of schools are willing to fund them. Indeed, the impact of the 1988 Act has made the adviser, and particularly the advisory teacher role, even more precarious, and recent changes in payment structures and levels will further exacerbate this. It is important therefore that LEAs seek to maximise the security of staff fulfilling advisory roles and are very clear in their dealings with prospective advisers about the prospects or otherwise of the job. Long term however, the future of an advisory service can only be guaranteed by its own effectiveness – if schools are to be the source of funding then schools will need to be convinced of the benefits which they derive from the adviser's work.

All the above difficulties can be tackled, though tackling them will be easier if the LEA adopts a systematic approach to adviser selection and training. Beyond that, personal effectiveness and the ability to support schools through rapid structural and curricular change will count heavily. Once the adviser has established the credentials to be invited into the schools, he/she will have to be able to demonstrate, via performance, why the school should repeat the invitation in the future.

It is here that the capacity to manage change will be tested. Key questions will include:

- was the school helped to confront the need for change?
- was a clearer definition of what specific changes would be aimed at evolved?
- was this better communicated and understood than previously?
- were all staff appropriately involved in planning and implementing the necessary changes?
- did staff commitment and morale improve?
- did external help simplify rather than complicate the process?
- does the school feel it has 'grown' as a result of the experience?

Where the answers to these questions are positive, advisory staff will find a future despite financial constraints, because they will then have become a priority for the school, rather than an adornment of the LEA. In such circumstances their influence will be authentic, their job satisfaction much increased, and the quality of schooling improved.

References

Audit Commission (1989) *Losing an Empire – Finding a Role:- the LEA of the Future*. London: HMSO.

Bolam, R. (1984) 'Some Practical Generalisations about the change process' in Campbell, G. (Ed.) *Health Education and Youth: A Review of Research and Development*. London: Ward Lock Educational.

Coopers and Lybrand, (1988) *Local Management of Schools: a Report to the DES*. London: Coopers and Lybrand.

Eraut, M. (1977) 'Some Perspectives on consultancy in in-service Education' in *British Journal of In-Service Education*. vol. 4: (2).

Everard, K. B. and Morris, E. (1985) *Effective School Management*. London: Harper and Row.

Everard, K. B. (1986) *Developing Management in School*. Oxford: Blackwell.

Fullan, M. and Park, P. (1981) *Curriculum Implementation*. Toronto: Ministry of Education.

Fullan, M. (1982) *The Meaning of Educational Change*. New York: Teachers' College Press.

Harland, J. (1990) Advisory Teachers: What do they do, How do they do it? in *TOPIC Autumn 1990*. Windsor: NFER.

Heller, H. (1985) *Helping Schools Change*. York: CSCS.

Heller, H. (1988) 'The Advisory Service and Consultancy' in Gray H. L. (Ed.) *Management Consultancy in Schools*. London: Cassell.

House of Commons (1988) *Education Reform Act 1988*.

Mulford, W. (1982) 'Consulting with Education Systems is about the Facilitation of Coordinated Effort' in Gray H. L. (Ed.) *The Management of Educational Institutions*. Lewes: Falmer.

Pearce, J. (1986) *Standards and the LEA: the Accountability of Schools*. Windsor: NFER.

Stillman, A. and Grant, M. (1989) *The LEA Adviser – a Changing Role*. Windsor: NFER.

West, M. and Ainscow, M. (1991) *Managing School Development*. London: David Fulton.

CHAPTER 9

Exploring the partnership between the LEA advisory and inspection service and schools

Ken Shooter and Mel West

Introduction

The role of the LEA advisory and inspection service, and its function in relation to the schools it serves, has been debated for decades, particularly at times of national change and development within the education service.

Most recently, the Education Reform Act 1988 has clearly emphasised the importance of the role of LEA advisory and inspection services in increased 'quality control' activities, and away from those activities (identified by Bolam et al., (1978)) which suggested that the main functions were advisory, inservice training and curriculum innovation. The dilemma of orientation, to advise or to inspect, has been with the service since its inception at the turn of this century. An example of this continuing problem was highlighted in a recent Annual Report of H.M. Senior Chief Inspector of Schools, which stated that many local advisory/inspection services were experiencing some difficulties in making the transition from advisory work to inspection, and in finding the appropriate balance. Indeed, some services because of this tension 'were cutting themselves off from relating inspection to advisory work' (DES 1989).

This chapter argues that despite the structural reorganisation which is taking place in a number of LEAs to separate out 'inspection'

132

and 'advice' functions, advisers will continue to have an important role to play in the development of schools. Even in those activities associated with formal inspection there are many opportunities for advisers to make constructive inputs into the analysis and decision-making processes of schools. However, if this contribution is to be maintained, then the *relationship* between advisers and schools will be critical – it must be an authentic partnership underpinned by mutual regard and trust.

There are two main sections in the chapter: the first is a brief historical survey of the changing functions of the service and its relationship with schools, in order to place what is happening currently in context; the second section explores opportunities for partnership provided by the Education Reform Act (1988), and the continuing struggle for balance between support and evaluation within this relationship. (Throughout this chapter the words adviser, and inspector are used to denote those members of the LEA service who have a clear monitoring function in relation to schools).

Influences on and Opportunities for Partnership – an historical perspective

The LEA Advisory Service has experienced a chequered development since its inception in the early part of this century. It was established officially following the Education Act of 1902, which established local education authorities and empowered them to 'promote the general co-ordination of all forms of education'. In those early years every aspect of school life was investigated by 'inspectors', who concentrated particularly on areas such as discipline, childrens' levels of attainment, auditing, attendance, punctuality, stockbooks, the state of the buildings and general efficiency in schools. Winkley (1985) suggests that from the outset a major problem for those early inspectors was to reconcile the dichotomy of being both an 'inquisitor' or 'snoop' and an adviser to teachers, so that trust and co-operation could be developed and a working partnership established which would benefit schools and pupils. This dilemma still exercises the minds of advisers.

A second influence on the advisory service came with the *Regulations for Secondary Schools* (1906/7), which extended the curriculum to include organised games, physical exercises, manual instruction, singing, and 'housewifery' for girls. These areas were outside the range of topics that were included in formal teacher training and a new breed of peripatetic support teacher was born, – the 'organiser or adviser' (paid at 'craftsman' rates) who moved from school to school providing instruction in these subjects. This development continued into the inter-war period. Local government records show that this group, together with 'inspectors', were responsible for developing the first forms of inservice training, largely in response to the needs of the schools in these practical subjects. Records also show that in Birmingham, the science and needlework organisers prepared lessons and the associated equipment on Fridays, to be distributed to schools for use the following week, often by untrained staff. This is probably the beginning of the LEA curriculum support service for schools as we recognise it. What is interesting, but not obvious, is that the initiative of providing support in this way did not come from central government but from the LEAs.

At a first glance, the 1944 Education Act does not appear to promote the partnership between LEA advisers and schools to any significant degree. However, a closer analysis of Section 77 (3), which gives LEAs the right to inspect their schools, reveals two important features which provide opportunities for the development of closer working relationships between this part of the LEA service and its schools.

First, this section of the Act validated the formation of the Advisory Inspection service, and second, it highlighted the need for each LEA to be responsible for *educational standards* in its schools and colleges. Unfortunately this latter duty was often interpreted by LEAs as a 'rolling programme' of general inspections, many of which were initially ill-conceived and without much consistency of purpose or criteria. This activity often alienated the advisers from schools. In fact, there was a considerable opportunity here to develop a system of quality control and monitoring which could be undertaken *jointly by schools and the LEA*, for the benefit of pupils and students, though sadly it was an opportunity which was largely overlooked.

In 1968, a Select Committee on Education and Science analysed the now much increased range of functions of LEA advisorates, and produced a report which clarified the type of support that schools and colleges could expect from the service. It extended the notion of 'inspecting and reporting on the work of schools and colleges,' by stating that this process entailed making suggestions to headteachers and teachers on improvements (in organisation, staffing, buildings, furniture and equipment) that might be made in light of the information provided by the inspection. In addition, it also high-lighted the importance of the adviser's role in 'stimulating interest in lively and creative approaches to education', such as organising and participating in courses and meetings for teachers, or arranging for teachers to see examples of good practice. The specialised subject or phase-related in-service element of the work of the LEA advisory and inspection service, which has been one of the most important ways of developing the partnership between schools and the service, grew out of this. In spite of the emphasis latterly on the generalist role, this is an area from which the service obtains much of its credibility, its perceived 'expertise' within specific curriculum or subject areas.

This report also identified the importance of several other functions which contributed to the working partnership. Among the more important of these were: 'supervising the work of teachers in their first appointments...; interviewing teachers seeking posts in the authority's schools...; transmitting information and views from the authority to teachers and from teacher to the authority...; guiding over considerable periods of time new developments in education...; and consulting with architects at local level in planning, furnishing and equipping of new schools'.

The Taylor report *A new partnership for our schools*, (1977) though focusing on the development of school governing bodies, concluded that partnership between the LEA, teachers, parents and pupils and the local community must be encouraged. It identified, as one aspect of the school governors' role, the responsibility for monitoring the rigour and quality of the learning process in partnership with professionals. It also clarified the importance of the development of this partnership in relation to LEA advisory/inspection services, stating that 'every local education authority should take steps to ensure that the services of a general adviser are regularly available to each of its schools, and that the general adviser will be available for consultation with and report to the governing body on request' (section 6.42).

Most recently, developments in the structure and control of the education service can be linked with *Better Schools* (1985). The role of LEA advisory/inspection services is no exception. In September 1985, Sir Keith Joseph, then Secretary of State for Education and Science, issued a draft statement on the role of LEA advisers and inspectors and 'the strategic part they have to play in securing improvements in standards which the policies in *Better Schools* are designed to achieve'.

This statement identified four interrelated groups of functions which were to be applied across the complete range of educational establishments, functions which underpinned the role that general advisers had to play, thus specifying the role advisers would hold between LEAs and schools.

These were:

   (i) 'Monitoring and evaluating the work of the Authority's Education Service through formal inspection processes, thematic evaluations, and by visiting schools regularly and on a less formal basis.'

   (ii) 'Work in support of schools and other establishments'. This statement confirmed the contribution that advisers make to educational innovation and development by working 'with teachers within individual schools, to initiate and promote curriculum development'.

   (iii) 'Supporting and developing teachers and advising on their management'... and 'giving direct support to individual teachers', in terms of career development and training needs.

   (iv) 'Work on local and national initiatives'. This function referred to planning and supporting the LEA's curriculum policy initiatives, and the adviser's role in relation to school re-organisations, responses to DES circulars, preparing ESG bids, and co-ordinating bids for the extension of TVEI.

The Secretary of State's overall statement was intended to stimulate LEAs into reviewing the role of the advisory service in the light of future demands.

In October 1989, following a substantial period of deliberation and consultation between the DES and LEAs about this role, the Audit Commission published the findings of a survey it had conducted into LEA advisory services during 1987/88, entitled *Assuring Quality in Education*. The survey revealed that 'the service's work covers the monitoring and evaluation of standards of work in schools and colleges, the provision and management support to these institutions, the provision of educational advice to the LEA's chief officer... and the provision of educational initiatives local to the LEA.'

In addition, it found that 'advisory work often extends to include the provision of in-service training (INSET) for teaching staff.... One major responsibility is overseeing the work of advisory teachers who work alongside school teachers in detailed development of curricular initiatives.'

The report also produced some recommendations on the main changes in direction that would be needed to help inspection and advisory services to fulfil the functions required of them as a result of the Education Reform Act (1988). These recommendations included:

'the development of more systematic monitoring',

with more intensive direct observation of teaching and learning and better record keeping, and 'active management of advice giving to ensure that advice is as soundly based and pertinent.'

The dual nature of the advisory role persists then, and it seems that the 1990s will bring continued tensions into the working lives of advisers and into their relationships with schools, as they seek to fulfil two main functions.

(1) To promote quality through monitoring, evaluation and inspection in all its forms.

(2) To provide specialist advice in the management of each phase of education, and in and across all aspects of the curriculum.

The remainder of the chapter will consider in some detail the implications of these functions for advisers and adviser – school relations in the context of the Education Reform Act.

Exploring the opportunities for partnership provided by the Education Reform Act 1988

1. The promotion of quality through monitoring, evaluation and inspection in all its forms

The 1988 Act has strengthened the case for monitoring and evaluation of schools by LEAs by providing a framework of explicit educational criteria against which schools' educational performance will be judged – the National Curriculum – and by giving schools responsibility for managing their own budgets. These measures combine to provide strong pressure for 'accountability' giving added emphasis to Section 77 of the Education Act 1944, which gave LEAs the right to carry out inspections and places an obligation on them to develop a 'strategic plan' for the education service.

In the context of the inspection and evaluation of a school's educational performance, it is important for the advisory service to look upon these processes as part of a continuum of longer term contact to develop the institution. In an increasing number of cases this is likely to involve objective critical analysis against clearly identified goals and targets which have been set out in the school development plan (SDP). But, whatever documentation about goals is available to inform the review process, the acid test for any policy on inspections remain, is it of real value to the establishment involved? (or, in the case of thematic evaluations, to a wider audience of LEA schools?)

A number of anxieties have been expressed about the ability of advisory services to engage in this kind of developmental dialogue, given the sheer volume of inspecting/reporting which seems to be required. For example, the Society of Chief Inspectors and Advisers, in a discussion document about LEA Services and the Education Reform Act, point out 'the new inspection and reporting duties of advisers leave little doubt that the support role is in danger of being marginalised by the weight of monitoring duties unless clear pro-active strategies are adopted.' (SCIA 1989). They also argue that evaluation should normally be a more dynamic activity than simply inspecting 'what is', suggesting that the process should draw not only on inspection data, but on regular advisory involvement with a school through all the phases of its planning and development. That this is likely to yield more durable and credible information which can be put to direct use in promoting the school's objectives and priorities is beyond dispute. That it can be managed within current resources is beyond belief – hence the anxiety.

Monitoring school performance

There are many possible approaches to monitoring, evaluation and inspection activities. Each one can be designed for particular situations, for a specific audience or range of audiences. However, the central purpose must always be the improvement of the quality of education for pupils. The most important audience therefore is likely to be made up from the teachers and governors of the school taking part. Indeed, although these processes are for the most part conducted by the LEA advisory service, i.e. an agency outside the school or schools, they cannot be carried out without the full cooperation of the staff within the school, and, therefore, monitoring needs to be developed as a joint enterprise. Without professional collaboration and a commitment to use the process to produce outcomes which directly benefit pupils, any monitoring will necessarily be narrow and tend towards checking and assessment. If the sense of 'checking' is communicated to the staff of the school, this in turn lessens the likelihood of collaboration, and reduces the effectiveness. It is important, therefore, to consider how the various forms of 'monitoring' can be used to support school development. The most frequently used are:

- systematic focused visiting of schools
- observation of teaching and learning

- thematic evaluation and cross LEA sampling and
- formal reviews, audits, evaluations and inspections of establishments

The implications of these for adviser/school relationships are considered below.

(i) Systematic focused visiting of schools

Over the years, the notion of a 'critical friend' to the school has been developed in many LEAs. Most recently, this development has been strengthened by the attachment of adviser/inspectors to particular schools, as LEAs have moved towards the so-called 'patch system'. Where LEAs are organised this way the adviser will probably be engaged in a programme of regular visits, mainly to see the head-teacher, but sometimes members of the governing body and other senior members of staff as appropriate. Within this relationship, a general adviser will be spending an increasing amount of time on issues which have arisen out of the Education Act (1988).

In this context two very important areas where monitoring evaluation and support are inseparable are:

- the review of the school development plan; and the school's annual curriculum return
- the analysis of results of National Examinations and National Curriculum assessment

These are areas where feedback to both the school and the LEA are vital, but the way in which data is collected and interpreted, and the form the feedback takes will be a major influence on the quality of relationships.

The school development plan is central to everything that makes a school an effective and efficient deliverer of education, and potentially can provide advisers with a method of obtaining for the LEA an 'up-to-date knowledge of the institutions it maintains' (Sir Keith Joseph, 1985). Equally as important, it provides an opportunity for the attached adviser to talk about and, with staff from the school, look at the school's current situation, its future plans, in order to place these in the framework of the demands of the Education Reform Act, LEA policies and the school's context.

Headteachers can be expected to welcome this opportunity to discuss the school's progress and plans so long as there is mutual trust and professional respect within the relationship – the adviser therefore must strive to establish the mutual interest of all partners in supporting the school.

In such a context, school development planning can become a more broadly collaborative activity, drawing in partners from beyond the school's boundaries. There is scope for Advisers to take the initiative here. In Cambridgeshire, for example, the Inspection Service has produced suggested guidelines for school development planning with some examples of the different ways that schools have produced plans. These are being used by the LEA's inspectors when they talk with heads and governors about carrying out school audits, drawing up plans and reviewing and reporting progress. They seem to provide a useful basis for discussions and this may also prove to be one way of breaking down one of the 'traditional' school/adviser barriers.

A problem faced by inspectors/advisers is building personal credibility within schools.

> They are most likely to do this if they are seen to be making a direct and positive contribution to school's consultative and decision making processes, rather than observing from a distance in a way that under-lines the 'us-them' relationship . . . They are also in the best position to encourage a balance between national, local and school priorities. During the audit stage of the School Development Plan, they may suggest areas that are in danger of being overlooked . . . can be a stimulus to more rigorous thinking and have an important role to play in encouraging schools to be more self-critical.
>
> (Holt 1990)

Though Holt's claims are rather sweeping, the point that participation leads to influence is worth under-lining.

A further opportunity for adviser collaboration arises in relation to the Schools Annual Curriculum return (ACR). Though not a formal requirement of the DES, this return which shows how teaching time is allocated to the various subjects, is of considerable interest to the LEA and to governors. Many headteachers, particularly those in smaller schools, could find the opportunity to discuss this with an adviser who has some knowledge of the school, as well as a wider picture of what is happening across the LEA, a beneficial process.

The second major element within the area of systematic sampling is the analysis of external examination results at 16+ or post 16. Each year, after these have been published, it is usual for the LEA's advisers to analyse these results to observe how the students have performed against local and national averages in subject areas, and to compare the overall performance within the school with results in preceding years. Of course, where such analysis gives cause for concern, this is likely to be a sensitive issue for the school. But it is, nevertheless, one which must be tackled. The adviser should be able to *help* the school to progress in such circumstances – remembering that it is the quality of the school's response which increases pupil performance. The emphasis, therefore, needs to be on exploring the problem of a constructive and supportive fashion, ensuring that the school knows how to call upon the various sets of expertise within the advisory service which may help, being prepared to participate with the school in analysing and planning for development in particular areas.

Most often, however, the dialogue between school and adviser will not be about identifying areas where improvement is necessary, but about how the school and its staff can learn and grow from the accumulating experience.

Of course, LEAs have a general duty under the National Curriculum to secure the implementation of assessment arrangements in the schools they maintain, and advisers will play an important part in monitoring and quality assurance in relation to the assessment processes in schools, particularly in comparing these with local and national monitoring standards. Programmes of systematic, focused sampling at appropriate times in the academic year by the adviser attached to each establishment, can fulfil the obligation and generate important discussion within the school if approached sensitively. They can also provide opportunities for positive feedback to schools.

(ii) Observation of teaching and learning situations

This activity can be instigated for a number of reasons within the context of monitoring and development. It can be part of an attached adviser's programme of regular visits to schools, when the length of the classroom visits will be relatively short and often in the form of a tour of part of the school in order to gain general impressions. Such visits will be informal, often unaccompanied, and create opportunities when advisers can give recognition and reassurance.

It is accepted professional practice for any adviser to notify the school of an intention to visit, so that when time is being allowed for a general tour, the head can notify the staff to expect the adviser to be around the building. But such visits are short and discussion with teachers and pupils tends to be limited because it is not desirable to disrupt teaching and learning processes.

Nevertheless, the support and motivation which can be provided by such visits needs stressing. Teachers obtain little feedback particularly about aspects of their work inside the classroom. It is an essential part of a visiting adviser's work to *recognise* achievement and effort, and to give praise which may help to maintain or raise morale within the school. There is also an opportunity to identify areas of classroom practice which may require attention or development but how comments on such areas can best be fed into the school needs careful thought. Teachers and headteachers alike value feedback from visiting advisers, where comments are objective, reasonable and constructive, and much may be achieved via informal observation and discussion.

Other visits may be made on a more formal basis. Teachers in their probationary year, licenced and articled teachers may be observed teaching complete lessons, upon which notes will be made by the adviser and then discussed afterwards with the teacher concerned. Such notes should cover individual professional strengths, and areas which demonstrate particular progress and good practice, in addition to aspects which may need further development. This type of observation may be the first time a new teacher has been formally monitored by someone who is not known to them and so can bring particular anxiety. It is, therefore, important for such teachers to know the criteria upon which they will be assessed, why reports are made, what they contain, and how they will be used. This is an opportunity for the adviser to establish a supportive relationship with the new teacher, such that the new teacher begins to recognise the benefits and value of a working partnership between the LEA advisorate, the teacher and the school. In addition, the adviser can also help to ensure that the school is fulfilling its responsibility to the new teacher in terms of assessment, reporting and support. S/he may also be able to advise the teacher (and the head) about other schools which are worth a visit, and of INSET opportunities which may be appropriate for a new teacher.

A different type of formal observation takes place in connection with establishment inspection, or LEA wide evaluation of specific themes. Here, arrangements are made for advisers to visit classrooms to observe teaching and learning in a variety of contexts and across a number of teaching groups and key stages. During such a process, the individual teacher's capability is not being assessed, as in the case of the new teacher in her/his probationary year (a fuller account of this aspect of monitoring and evaluation will be examined under formal inspections) but the relationship between teacher and adviser is equally important.

However, there is another type of formal classroom observation made by advisers which is concerned with the individual teacher's capability. This occurs when a headteacher has embarked on a disciplinary procedure with a teacher on the grounds of suspected lack of capability or competence. In this context the adviser acts as a specialist observer, and, in the first instance, as a consultant on the support needed and the steps which need to be taken by the teacher to improve. Subsequently, the adviser may act as a neutral witness if and when the head decides that disciplinary procedures should be formally instigated. It should be stressed that where advisers are requested by headteachers to observe teachers in this situation and to make recommendations, they do so in a completely neutral capacity, and not merely to reinforce the head's case against the teacher. All reports on such observations should be seen by and discussed with the teacher whose capability is being questioned. The first question should always be, what support can the school and the LEA give the teacher in order to remediate identified weaknesses?

(iii) Thematic evaluations and cross-LEA sampling

The phrase 'eyes and ears of the education service' is a familiar one in terms of the monitoring and evaluation role of advisers. The collection and analysis of information and data is becoming an accepted role and has been touched upon in the section on systematic, focused visiting. Thematic evaluation and cross-LEA sampling is a formally organised process through which the LEA attempts to discover what is happening across a range of its schools. The implementation of the National Curriculum in the LEA's schools for example, or schools' procedures for assessing and recording pupils achievements are possible areas for such monitoring activities. When contemplating this sort of evaluation, it is again important to establish a partnership between adviser and school. This means that such a process requires careful preparation, with joint planning, agreed procedures, clear coordination and reporting arrangements. One of the main objectives must be to provide participating schools with feedback on their own (including good!) practice. The audience may also extend to other LEA schools, so that those not involved in the survey can learn from the findings. Sharing the end-product, i.e. information which has been gathered objectively, analysed and presented in a way which is relevant but where individual schools are not identified by name, is a positive form of evaluation which can demonstrate the usefulness of monitoring by an outside agency.

The production of a report is, however, not the end-product, nor indeed the main reason for such evaluations. Unlike HMI, advisers are generally known to the schools they serve, and have to continue working with them after reports have been issued and discussed. The processes of monitoring, of evaluation and inspection may service several functions. They can, for example, provide information on the strengths and weaknesses of management and organisation, on how pupils are performing compared with other similar schools, on the levels of resourcing in physical and human terms, compared with general patterns. They may also suggest what the priorities for development should be. But they are nevertheless only part of the continuing and sustained relationship an adviser needs with her/his schools. Thus after such evaluations, the advisorate shares the responsibility for development with the school. This will involve the fostering of good practice, strengthening areas of deficiency, and bringing to the LEA's attention any constraints which may be inhibiting the school(s) from performing effectively e.g. inappropriate facilities, low levels of funding, poor resourcing or staffing difficulties.

(iv) Formal 'reviews', 'audits', 'evaluations' and other types of inspections of individual establishments

There are several kinds of external inspection which fall into this category and which may concentrate on the whole or on part of an establishment. There is, however, currently a debate about the value and rationale behind the notion of the full inspection, in terms of its effectiveness and of the best use of the advisorate's time. Many LEAs are moving away from programmes in which the full inspection of an establishment is a regular feature, and moving towards a more focused evaluation strategy. However, whatever the LEA policy, the methodological issues and hence the opportunities for working jointly with schools towards improvements in the quality of education, remain the same.

Although the inspection is an 'external evaluation', the process cannot proceed or indeed have much effect without the cooperation of the staff of the establishment. This is particularly true of the whole-establishment inspection. Pickles (1986) has pointed out that where the inspection is not seen as relevant to the school's situation, this can usually be traced to a lack of cooperation and coordination at the planning stage.

The well established method of the school inspection carried out by . . . local authority advisers usually highlights matters of use to the school, . . . when it does not, it may be because the school was not ready for it, or that the purposes had not been adequately explained or simply that the issues of concern to those inspecting were not shared by the teachers in the school.

(Pickles 1986)

Depending on the reasons for the inspection, and its objectives, there are a number of aspects on which the advisorate and the school or college must work together, for best effect.

First, the establishment involved needs to know the criteria on which the inspection is to be based, so that they understand what advisers are looking at and for, and against what benchmarks they will make judgements.

Second, in addition to the specific information on and details of such aspects as school policies, organisational structures, staffing and curriculum matters which are requested prior to the actual inspection visit, staff in the school should be given the opportunity to offer further supportive information which may be relevant and provide a more informed perspective on the areas being analysed.

Third, when the classroom visits and/or meetings with staff are being planned it is an advantage to consult senior and/or middle management on the convenience and appropriateness of such activities. If advisers indicate clearly what they want to do and see, and plan this collaboratively, then tensions can often be avoided, the usefulness of the visits enhanced, and disruption to normal school activities minimised. Only by working with staff in this way, can time be used efficiently and to maximum effect.

Fourth, after such visits, particularly where classroom observation is involved, feedback should be provided by advisers and opportunities provided for discussion, *as soon as practicable*. This gives the adviser an opportunity to check on the accuracy of her/his observations and any interpretations made from these observations, which inevitably can only be a limited 'snapshot' of practice. It also allows the teacher(s) to clarify any aspects of uncertainty.

After the report has been produced, often after a draft copy has again been checked for accuracy and objectivity with staff, the establishment can formulate an action plan to build on strengths and focus on areas which require development. Nothing in a report should come as a surprise to the school or college staff. Where professional collaboration has been a feature of the inspection process and both sides have been objective and honest then the support process by the advisorate for the establishment's action plan can be expected to be effective and appropriate. Where the two have not worked together, the inspection process may have been dogged by suspicion and conflict within the school or college. Then the establishment will feel no ownership of the evaluation, and a correspondingly low commitment to improve in even areas of identified weakness. Without collaboration then, inspection will be a sterile process. Goodwill between advisers and teachers is at the core of constructive evaluation.

2. Providing specialist advice in the management of each phase of education, and in and across all aspects of the curriculum

Addressing the challenges to the education system brought about by recent legislation, the Audit Commission have (in an occasional paper) stated that the 'LEA is central to the success of the reform package'. Considering the scope for LEA support in the new context, the paper argues that a new partnership will be required. As 'partner' to schools, LEAs will need to recognise that the scope of their 'advice' to schools will need to be reconsidered:

Specifically, schools and colleges will need help and guidance in:

- delivering the curriculum
- allocating and controlling the financial resources at their disposal
- making best use of human resources; and
- development planning

(Audit Commission 1989(2))

These suggestions provide a useful framework within which to analyse the potential contribution of advisers in supporting schools and colleges through the provision of specialist advice in its many forms. We will consider each of these in turn.

(i) Delivering the curriculum

The focus of support for the curriculum will evolve from the LEA's own curriculum policy, which should state clearly the values upon which its education service is based. From these (typically) broad statements more detailed guidance will need to be produced for specific curriculum areas, and advisers can play a key role here. Many LEAs have already drawn upon advisory staff to produce materials which support the introduction of National Curriculum core and foundation subjects, and also help develop cross-curricular awareness. Such materials are being used in LEA subject-based in-service education and training, and have also been distributed to schools for use within their own professional development activities. As well as creating resources for schools, advisers may play an important 'interpretative' role here, by producing clear guidance on the requirements of the Education Reform Act. This interpretative role has at least two aspects. First, 'translating' the regulations

> It shall be the duty . . . (c) of every governing body or headteacher of a maintained school as respects that school; to exercise their functions (including, in particular, the functions conferred on them by this chapter with respect to religious worship and the National Curriculum) with a view to securing that the curriculum for the school satisfies the requirements of this section.
>
> (Education Reform Act 1988)

Clearly there is a place for commentaries on the Act which are expressed in terms more accessible to governors, heads and teachers. Second, advisers can do much to link the various sections of the Act with the bewildering range of additional publications which need to be assimilated alongside it. These include publications from the National Curriculum Council, the range of DES circulars which highlight aspects of the curriculum, of assessment, or supply additional information, 'explain' temporary exemptions for individual pupils etc. and the Statutory Orders for National Curriculum subjects.

Such documents have poured onto headteachers' desks since the Act with unrelenting regularity. Not only is it difficult for schools to keep pace with all the new regulations, but teachers and governors need to be supported and provided with relevant training in order to understand the legislation and act upon it. Meetings and in-service opportunities organised by the advisorate, where such regulations can be explained, discussions between a school's attached adviser and staff groups, contact between subject advisers and individual subject specialists all offer important support mechanisms. These are clear examples of how advisers and teachers working together can help schools to come to terms with the changes.

More broadly, as the Audit Commission paper, Assuring Quality in Education (1989(2)) points out, 'the advisory service can alert a governing body to local and national educational developments relevant to its particular circumstance'. Advisers should also therefore play a part in informing and (perhaps) training governors on curriculum issues, thereby extending the collaborative working partnership which will be needed as the full effects of the Act are experienced. Governors in turn should recognise that they have access to professional guidance from advisers on matters concerned with the curriculum as well as the school.

(ii) Allocating and controlling the financial resources at their disposal

The process of financial delegation to schools and colleges will undoubtedly bring about considerable changes in the ways these establishments are managed and alter adviser influence. Hitherto, advisers have often been able to influence curriculum development in schools through the specific control and distribution of LEA resources. Under the Act this direct influence largely disappears. However, LEAs still have a responsibility for ensuring that *all pupils* are being educated satisfactorily, and that delegated funding and resources are being used effectively to this end. Heads, particularly in primary schools, may well look for guidance and support in managing delegated budgets. Though such advice will often come from specialist LMS teams, advisers need to be aware of the problems that schools face as they enter the LEA's scheme of delegated funding. The attached adviser can keep track of such issues in the regular meetings with the head, and will be able to discuss and offer advice on such matters as appropriate levels of resourcing, staffing and responsibility allowances in the light of the National Curriculum and LEA policies. Where specialised help is required the adviser may be in a position to draw this to the attention of the LEA's LMS support staff, or to recommend that a specialist subject adviser visits the school to talk with the head and other staff about particular concerns. This is one example of the very important role of 'facilitator' that the attached adviser can fulfil.

However, there is no doubt that the adviser too will be on a steep learning curve in terms of understanding how LMS will effect schools and the challenges and opportunities it can present headteachers. An honest working relationship between attached advisers and heads will help the professional development of both partners in this new area. In order to provide feedback to the LEA, advisers will also need to gain an understanding of the attitudes of heads and principals to the LEA's scheme and how it is being supported, particularly their views on any discretionary exceptions made by the LEA from the general schools budget. They should also keep a 'weather eye' on any conflicts between governors and headteachers.

As the scheme is fully implemented, headteachers may require individual help and guidance from the LEA through the attached adviser, in respect of the new arrangements within the School Teachers' Pay and Conditions of Employment legislation (1990) for incremental enhancement, for example, or on the criteria for rewarding incentive allowances, or spot salaries for unqualified teachers. These issues will come into sharper focus as governors become the 'relevant body' for such negotiations, and heads too can negotiate enhancement of their salaries within the groups and ranges provided by the regulations. There may also be occasions when the head will value help in explaining certain statutory responsibilities to the governing body in relation to its decisions about funding and priorities.

In addition, at the secondary phase, the specialist adviser may be called upon to plan in-service training courses which raise the awareness of subject co-ordinators and heads of department about the impact of LMS on the way they manage their own areas of responsibility.

As the LEA's representative, the adviser also has a responsibility to take an interest in the way schools manage their financial resources. This function may be reflected in a formally organised programme of sampling and monitoring across the LEA's schools, but it is a function which needs to be carefully managed, if an active partnership is to be promoted. Advisers need to ensure that their more general interest in how school's deploy resources to promote pupil learning is not 'contaminated' by this 'checking' activity.

(iii) Making best use of human resources

The requirements of the National Curriculum mean that certain subjects and areas of study will have priority in the allocation of resources at certain times, as the National Curriculum is implemented. Advisers, in their general and specialised roles, will need to discuss with heads and subject co-ordinators how this can best be achieved, within the opportunities and constraints of funding available, and in such a way that the 'whole curriculum' is also protected.

As more GEST funding is delegated to schools and colleges for in-service training, advice will also be needed on the most appropriate forms of staff development, which will be of maximum benefit to the schools and professional development of individual teachers. There is no doubt that the element of support through the provision of adviser planned, LEA-based in-service training will need a competitive edge in terms of its relevance and quality, as schools have more access to more delegated funding, but if advisers stay attuned to the priorities of their schools and teachers, they should not fear competition. Additionally, they may become a useful source of advice to schools on how to get best value from INSET providers.

Schools also need advice on the appropriateness and safety of equipment and materials that suppliers are marketing. Manufacturers have seen the opportunities presented by such new subjects as Technology, and are engaged in high pressure advertising directly to schools. Both senior and middle management need help in recognising value for money when purchasing teaching and learning resources. Advisers with specialist knowledge of subject requirements should be able to find ways of helping schools through this maze. Many LEAs, through their advisorates, publish helpful guidelines for schools on acquiring appropriate classroom resources. Others will organise advisory and curriculum support teachers who will offer practical support to schools.

(iv) 'Development and planning'

The school development plan (SDP) is at the heart of the school's decision-making process. Review, identifying priorities, planning and monitoring merge into a continuous cycle in the SDP, the focus of which must be quality of experience in the classroom. This process, though it will have particular attention at particular points, spreads throughout the year and provides a framework in which other aspects of a working partnership between heads and attached advisers may evolve. Throughout the year, advisers will want to refer to the plan as a focus for disucssion with the head about the school's progress and development, particularly relating to staffing and the allocation of funding to areas of need. As a 'critical friend' the adviser should be able to discuss with the school how progress can best be monitored and evaluated, perhaps based on an agreed set of 'performance indicators'. If this collaborative enterprise is working effectively, there should be no surprises at times of formal review of the development plan by the LEA, and all parties, including staff and governors, should be familiar with the contents.

Finally, aspects of Health and Safety legislation also fall within the compass of the area of development and planning. Headteachers and governors have a responsibility to work within the Health and Safety at Work Act (1974) and subsequent provisions. Specialist subject advisers can provide an informed source of advice for heads and heads of department on issues connected with specific areas, and they can assist with appropriate in-service courses to explain new legislation and procedures. In some LEAs, advisers carry out safety checks for subject departments where concern is expressed by the school or another visiting officer of the LEA, and though not a major aspect of the role, it is one which needs to be taken seriously by all parties.

Conclusion

This chapter has explored the opportunities for the development of a working partnership between the LEA advisory and inspection services and schools. It has attempted to demonstrate that the dual functions of support and evaluation are not incompatible, but are complementary activities if tackled with mutual respect and goodwill.

At a local level, much will depend on the ability of the service to understand the needs of and new demands being placed on its schools, particularly in the light of the 1988 Act, and the degree to which advisers can help them respond effectively to these pressures. In this context there are a wide variety of roles which the adviser/inspector can undertake, e.g. external evaluator, critical friend, catalyst, consultant, arbitrator and neutral expert witness. What will be important is the ability of advisers to fulfil particular roles at particular times, as the occasion demands, and to switch roles without losing credibility.

Even where formal monitoring or inspection is required, or when reporting to governing bodies on the quality of teaching and learning in a particular school or college, the advisorate, to be effective, should be seen as a partner, *working with staff* to promote good practice and quality assurance. If, as a consequence of recent legislation, the advisorate distances itself from teachers and becomes a body which concentrates solely on inspection, monitoring and report-writing, the relationship which has been built on teamwork and collaboration over half a century will be lost, and children in our schools will be the losers.

152

References

Audit Commission (1989)(1) Occasional Paper No. 10 *Losing an Empire, Finding a Role: The LEA of the Future*. London: HMSO.

Audit Commission (1989)(2) *Assuring Quality in Education: The role of the Local Education Authority Inspectors and Advisers*. London: HMSO.

Bolam, R., Smith, G. and Canter, H. (1987) *LEA Advisers and the Mechanism of Innovation*. Windsor: NFER.

DES (1985) *Better Schools*. London: HMSO.

House of Commons (1988) *Education Reform Act*. London: HMSO.

DES (1985) *Education Services Should Be Reviewed: A Draft Statement*. DES.

Holt, K. 'Monitoring Evaluation: Some Thoughts' in Gilbert (1990) *Local Management of Schools*. London: Kogan Page.

House of Commons Select Committee (1968) *Report Part I, Her Majesty's Inspectorate*. London: HMSO.

H M Senior Chief Inspector of Schools (1990) *Standards in Education 1988–89*. D.E.S.

Pickles, H. 'Action Research: an LEA Adviser's view' in Hustler, Cassidy and Cuff (eds) (1966) *Action Research in Classrooms and Schools*. London: Allen and Unwin.

Society of Chief Inspectors and Advisers (1989) *LEA Advisory Services and the Education Reform Act 1988* S.C.I.A.

Taylor Report (1977) *A New Partnership for our Schools*. London: HMSO.

Winkley, D. (1985) *Diplomats and Detectives*. London: Robert Royce.

Index

154